Cage Liners

Stories about pets, vets, owners and other animals

Robert Hart

Other titles by Robert Hart

Hart's Original Petpourri
Oliver's Rubáiyát

Copyright © 2014 Robert Hart

ISBN: 149607596X
ISBN-13: 978-1496075963

Thank you, Veronica—

"Where there is love there is life."
Mahatma Gandhi

Cage Liners

Robert Hart

Contents

Acknowledgements
Introduction

1.	Paddling with Piglets	1
2.	How did I get this far?	5
3.	Where am I?	9
4.	Pulling the Wool over Their Eyes	12
5.	The Highland Fling	16
6.	Pig Iron	21
7.	An Udder Problem	24
8.	A Matter of Learning	32
9.	Proud Graduate	37
10.	Pygmy Cabbages	41
11.	Dammit Takes Tea	46
12.	That's Life	49
13.	Bare Skin	54
14.	Worm of a Different Scale	57
15.	The Break	64
16.	Sammi	69
17.	Spacey Medicine	72
18.	Footling Around	80
19.	Cat Speak	85
20.	One for You, One for Me	89
21.	Temperature Rising	95
22.	Shopping at Night	97
23.	The Office Call	101
24.	A Peach of a Case	104
25.	A Question of Memory	110
26.	Tartan Coat Syndrome	113
27.	"You Know…"	118
28.	The Silence of the Hams	122
29.	A Weighty Issue	129
30.	Two Ladies of Girth	135
31.	Quid pro Quo	141
32.	Hidden Memories	145
33.	Squashed	150
34.	Without a Cry	155
35.	Unintended Consequences	161
36.	Manic Monday	167

37.	Troublesome Tuesday	174
38.	And it's only Wednesday!	179
39.	The Doberman	187
40.	Thursday—Day of Rest	190
41.	Frantic Friday	193
42.	Saturday Morning	198
43.	Skunk Pursuit	202
44.	I am Oliver and I am a Cat	206

Previously published

Chapter 5, The Highland Fling, *Veterinary Technician*, 12, #3, 1991

Chapter 8, A Matter of Learning first appeared as *A Matter of Technique*, in *Veterinary Technician*, 12, #3, 1991

Chapter 16, Sammi first appeared as *One Friday Morning*, in *Dog World*, 69, #12, 1984

Chapter 17, Spacey Medicine, *Veterinary Technician*, 11, #5, 1990

Chapter 23, The Office Call, *Veterinary Technician*, 10, #9, *1989*

Chapter 26, The Tartan Coat Syndrome, *Veterinary Technician*, 11, #5, 1990

Chapter 42, Saturday Morning, *Veterinary Technician*, 10, #9, 1989

Chapter 44, I am Oliver, and I am a Cat, *The Florida Writer*, 3, # 1, p 31, winter 2009.

Acknowledgements

If you think there is good in everybody, you haven't met everybody. ~
Everything I Know I Learned in Corporate America

 Although this admission is painful, I admit I cannot remember all the relatives, clients, teachers, patients, colleagues and friends who have contributed to my fifty years in the veterinary profession. Too many brain cells lie discarded in the dust of experience. Each carries a memory now lost—some rightfully so. To those who remember helping me, take a bow and accept my thanks. To those missing from the action, please accept my apologies—the voyage was better for your company—it could not have been travelled without you.
 There are those I do remember and must recognize—obviously parents, or I wouldn't have been here, but mainly Veronica, my incredibly supportive wife. She reads everything I write, comments on, corrects and improves my shortcomings, whilst keeping me housed and fed like a humorously tolerated pet.
 I thank also my friends in the City Island Fiction Writers critique group of Daytona Beach, who offered corrections and suggested punctuation marks in the most ill-advised places.

Introduction

Get your facts first, then you can distort them as you please. ~ Mark Twain

Veterinarians often line their hospital pet-cages with newspaper, or place newspaper under a blanket, because it is easily discarded when soiled. This suggested an eco-title for these vignettes, Cage Liners, which can be recycled in pet cages after reading.

Written for entertainment, everything is based on incidents that actually happened. I have tried to let each stand alone, occasionally using a linking narrative to keep them flowing. I did not want this to be an autobiography, or to concentrate on treating clinical cases, although both were hard to avoid. The stories are more about people and how our interactions shaped my confused and sometimes irrational behavior. Apart from the early chapters I have mingled time and place since situations faced later in life often trigger memories of early experiences. And make one blush.

Most animal names have been changed to protect them from embarrassment. If you find a human character in the book that bears any relation to you, or someone you know, you may draw your own conclusions.

In addition to the wonderful animals and the interesting people that I have met over the years, my thanks and apologies are due to Aunt Josephine for her unwavering guidance.

My apologies to all our Aunt Josephines. She is an author's ploy, a composite of several people in one character for dramatic effect (and to save space). The more I have written about her, the more I have grown to like her. After all, to be in the presence of someone unashamedly self-righteous, shows us how remarkable and open minded we are. It is much like hiring the incompetent to make oneself appear brilliant, or looking for pictures of ugly people to make one feel fabulous!

1

Paddling with Piglets

There's nothing like castrating twenty pigs before lunch. ~ Fred Ward

How had it come to this?

I sloshed around in the pig pen trying to keep my balance on the concrete floor made slippery with urine and pig dung. A couple of dozen highly mobile piglets milled around, squealing about my feet. I reached forward, grabbed a hind leg, swung the little porker between my knees and presented its hind end to Alan Saunders, the veterinarian I was assisting on this farm visit.

The final clinical year of veterinary school covered four semesters from September until the December of the following year, thus including two summer vacations. During this period, the worthies governing our profession deemed it necessary that students spend vacations with a veterinarian who treated farm animals. This extra-mural study, with the inspired title of 'Seeing Practice,' covered a minimum of six months, thus my presence with Alan Saunders in the heady excitement and excrement of my first farm call.

We were castrating the males in a litter of piglets. The pork from adult male pigs develops a strong 'gamey' flavor unless the poor fellow has been reduced to eunuch status early in life. We were thus obliging the demands of the pork-eating public for an acceptable roast or future bacon slice. It is a simple procedure, crude in execution, dictated by economics, and, I believe, not appreciated by the pigs.

Gripping the creatures, slippery as oily eels, I let the vet do his stuff, remove the testicles and ensure that this piglet's genes, which evolved over thousands of years, would not pass to another generation. Each little fellow now destined to satisfy many a breakfast appetite. I handed the altered piglet over the wall to the farmer and grabbed the next.

Four years of studying animal husbandry in classes covering all the major aspects of farming had not touched on the reality of such pig rearing details. My pig books showed splendid posed pictures of breeds from Tamworth to Large White, discussed pig rearing methods, described the purpose and method of porcine surgical castration, but carefully left out such 'on-site features' as the digested pig food that lapped over my shoes and oozed into them, sliding down between the rich leather and my fine argyle socks. Miller's Practical Animal Husbandry, a 640-page tome on animal management, dismissed pig castration in three and a half lines slipped into the 'Handling' section, between the restraint of sheep and management of dogs, a small spurt of practical guidance aimed seemingly at random, like the liquid material squirting out of the hind end of these piglets.

"You have joined the profession from the moment you entered this college," our esteemed Professor of Surgery told us in our first lecture by almost five years before. "You will be expected to behave accordingly and in a professional manner."

As innocent as a piglet fated for the table, I had taken him at his word when he repeatedly told us in our clinical training that veterinarians were 'qualified men,' presumably to enhance our self esteem after our arduous course of study. He believed in the saying that 'clothes make the man'—I think he had a brother in the clothing trade—"You are professional men; dress accordingly," he admonished us—along with the aforementioned 'correct' behavior. This dutiful student listened, and so, for my summer experience, since I hadn't a clue what to expect, I had bought new clothes—a rather spiffy sports jacket, Harris Tweed in an appropriate hound's-tooth pattern, decent corduroy pants, and brown brogue shoes to match. And of course the argyle socks.

Alan Saunders said nothing when I had appeared earlier that morning, a picture of sartorial elegance that would have done our professor proud. But his eyes had glinted, I thought in admiration of my professional appearance. He did mention casually that I would find experience a great teacher, and then he trotted off to the car. Not getting the hint, I did not change clothes before this particular call.

My mentor led the way to the pig house, although I am quite sure I would have found it easily by following the rich gag-inducing smell of pig dung. The building, a long low windowless brick structure, housed a series of pens on either side of wide central passageway. A large fan hummed in the wall at the far end, though it did little to reduce the odor. This building bore little resemblance to the pristine housing provided for the pigs on the veterinary school farm.

Alan introduced me to Jonas Withins, the owner of the farm. He leaned against the wall of a pen, biting on his hand, staring at me with eyes crinkled in apparent astonishment. He appeared to have trouble talking.

"From the city are you?" he asked.

I nodded.

"Thought so."

Seized with a fit of coughing he turned away. Instinctively I knew something was wrong. Then I looked into the pig-pen. My face must have shown the shock I felt when I saw the animals crammed together. Between the small bodies I saw the floor awash with several inches of liquid pig dung. My heart would have been in my boots, but I didn't have any boots.

"Ready then?" Alan Saunders asked.

Not to seem the city sissy, I jumped into the pen.

I tried to ignore the growing wetness as the muck oozed through my trousers. I tried to ignore the squelching in my shoes. I tried to ignore the effect of wiping dung-slippery hands on my corduroys. I tried to ignore the tightness in my stomach. I allowed myself to focus on the job in hand, grab the hind legs, swing the pig between my knees, turn it towards Alan Saunders, hand it to Jonas Withins.

The hot glow of my cheeks, flushed from humiliation and embarrassment at my own stupidity, made my eyes water. Thankfully it also masked surprising feelings of revulsion, and a nagging worry about the brutality of what we were doing. These feelings I kept to myself. They concerned me because after investing years of study to become a veterinarian, I found myself harboring doubts that it may all have been a big mistake.

Like many things in life, trying to reconcile the reality of experience with idealistic expectations, created an inner conflict. I hoped that life would improve from here—hopes tempered by thoughts of ever bigger dung piles.

After the last little pig had completed this next step on the road to market, avoiding the looks of Saunders and Withins, I slunk out of the pen. Luckily I didn't throw up over the piglets to add to the mess.

Sensibly I had left tie and jacket in the car. Shoes and trousers were beyond redemption. That afternoon I bought replacements, plus rubber boots and coveralls. Transformed from the sartorial model preferred by the professorial directive, I looked at least functional. And I wouldn't raise eyebrows on any further calls. Well, that's what I thought.

I can grin now at the memories of my naïveté, and wonder why Alan and Withins didn't laugh out loud. I think, had they not been scheduled to be eaten, the piglets would have too.

2

How Did I Come This Far?

When the journey's over there'll be time enough to sleep. ~ A. E. Housman

The journey to the point in my veterinary education where I paddled with the piglets had been long, and at times convoluted, exasperating and baffling. It began in high-school almost a decade earlier. Naïve, and unfamiliar with real life, I did not suspect the maze of academic pitfalls and the fascinating warped logic of official government channels that faced me as a student 'from the colonies.' Our school principal asked how I intended to waste my life once I left the protective walls of the boarding school where I had spent the previous six years. I told him of my intention to become a Veterinary Surgeon. His reply was a foretaste of the life lessons to come.

"Can you spell it?"

Really, if the truth must be told, and this book is based on truth, I should add reaching a decision about a career was a gradual process. I had been interested in medicine for many years, and conditioned by where I grew up.

I lived in the British colonial African countries that are now recognized in their own right—Tanzania, Malawi and Swaziland. Expatriate living in those far-off days was divided between the luxuries of being able to afford a way of life far in excess of that which one might experience for the same income in post-WW2 Britain. We were able to afford cooks, gardeners and house staff, yet at the same time lacked common amenities taken for granted at home in England.

For several years, living in the rural areas of the countries, my father employed someone to carry water from a stream half-a-mile away and pour it into a tank on the roof—a couple of re-cycled fifty-five gallon oil drums. We cooked and heated water on a wood stove, lit the house with kerosene lamps, boiled and filtered our drinking water, processed toilet waste in a septic tank and used 'gray' water to irrigate a garden. Garbage cans were held fast by metal stakes to prevent hyenas from scavenging in them. At sundown, windows were closed, mosquito nets lowered over the beds, and the house sprayed with Flit ®, an oily, smelly, petroleum based insecticide to fight malarial carrying mosquitoes. And we wanted to live there? Had I been from a different culture I might have said, "Oy."

The way of life created a strange mixture of dependence and self-sufficiency. It also provided an environment shared with animals. At night I listened to the less domesticated ones roar, squeal or bark as they hunted, fought each other or courted mates. By day I busied myself with our horses, pet dogs, and sundry wounded or abandoned wildlife in rehab around the house. Green movement supporters would have envied our communion with nature.

Adding the cloistered environment of a boarding school in Swaziland for nine months of the year completed the preparation for a good dose of culture shock on my eventual return to the British Isles.

Ours was a church school, Protestant, private, and expensive, where, like Thomas Arnold, a famous former headmaster of Rugby school from 1828 – 1841, parents expected their offspring to learn 'First, religious and moral principles; second, gentlemanly conduct; third, intellectual ability'. Luckily they didn't notice the *protest* in Protestantism. I am not sure my parents thought this way. They sent me there to learn to ride a horse. Who could doubt that it was a sound parental reason—certainly one I appreciated.

We were expected to be clairvoyant at school. No one had bothered to write a code of rules to guide or control our behavior. Staff believed students possessed an inborn ability to know and distinguish right from wrong. We preferred to respect the 11th commandment, "Thou shalt not be found out." That such a spirit of moral freedom existed before the behavioral revolution of the sixties now seems remarkable. In addition, my self reliance was fostered by making a three day, 1200 mile, journey on my own between home and boarding school six times a year from the age of eleven. There was no alternative.

Learning to ride also meant time spent working with the horses in other ways, particularly those sick or injured. I also developed a love of racing which my parents encouraged by entering horses for me to ride in our local turf club meets which included flat races, hurdle races and steeple-chases.

I applied to all the universities in Britain that had veterinary schools—at that time seven. Except for Trinity College, Dublin, they replied that my level of academic education did not meet the entry requirements, probably because 'intellectual abilities' ranked third on the table of expectations. Trinity accepted me for a pre-veterinary year with one minor glitch—depending on the number of freshman veterinary students that passed first year, I may not have a place the second (sophomore) year.

On my way to Dublin, I checked my application with the Royal Veterinary College in London. On receiving my application two years before, the college had forwarded it to the Colonial Office because I lived in the colonies. Having never heard of me, and not being bothered enough to find out, my application was shelved in a government pigeonhole. However they resuscitated the application, I completed the formalities, and received a provisional place in the RVC, provided I completed the educational requirements to satisfy the University of London.

I completed my first year in Dublin. Then we parted company. London accepted my freshman year, which included chemistry, physics, biology and English, as equivalent to high-school standards—good enough to let me in. However the university worthies insisted I start over as a freshman. The veterinary course lasted five and a half years. I added a year to finalize a degree in Physiology, worked nearly two years as a house surgeon—technically an Assistant Lecturer in Surgery—the lowest rung on the ladder, followed by two more years divided between working in a veterinary school and studying in the anesthesia department of a medical school.

The journey is never over; there is never time to sleep.

3

Where am I?

I have never let my schooling interfere with my education. ~ Mark Twain

I had met Alan Saunders when I was still at high school. He had changed little from the veterinarian I remembered from meetings of the Nyasaland (Malawi) Turf Club when he had been the veterinarian on duty and I rode as an amateur jockey.

A slim man, 12 years my senior, Alan's hairline receded slightly above a face weathered from an open-air life. I sensed an aura of energy radiating from him when he bustled at a trot between the surgery—a converted garage—and his house. Usually he wore a jacket and tie which would have pleased our professor—he kept his coveralls in the car—complemented by large, black Wellington boots.

His practice nestled in a small market village surrounded by the gentle countryside of Devon. This county in the southwest of England was home to historic villages such as Sticklepath, Taw Green and Sampford Courtnay, strange and exotic sounding to a Colonial transplant. Although I expect to their inhabitants, African names sounded equally strange—Zomba, Limbe, or Chikwawa in the highlands of Malawi where we had both lived when I had started my veterinary journey, or Hlatikulu, Mbuluzi, and Mbabane in the hills and valleys of Swaziland where I finished my secondary school education.

I had experienced large animal practice before, both on

a large ranch in the low-veldt of Swaziland owned by our school principal, and during several vacations spent in the Government Veterinary Department in Blantyre, the largest town in the southern part of Nyasaland (Malawi). Neither bore any comparison to the British scene.

The stock on our principal's ranch, spread out over 40 square miles, more than 26,000 acres, had little contact with humans. The land was divided into six sections, the stock in each section being dipped on a weekly schedule in an insecticide to control skin parasites, particularly tick-borne diseases. For the staff, this meant in effect that rounding up semi-wild cattle, and dipping them, was a daily practice.

Medical practice on the ranch was rough and ready. The opportunity was taken during each dipping session to apply rough treatment to infected and fly-blown wounds by cleaning out with a crude tool made from stiff fencing wire, packing the lesion with antiseptic powder, and coating with Stockholm Tar, a product more usually painted on horse's hooves to prevent drying and cracking. The difficulty, activity and danger, combined with the bellows of terrified cattle, created a general air of mayhem that blinded one to the crudity of the procedures.

The Colonial Government veterinarians in Nyasaland were responsible for herd health in addition to treating individual animals. They assayed the strength of tick dips, vaccinated cattle, treated the sick and also manned a small-animal clinic. Unlike a regular British practice, the department had full pathology facilities, diagnostic facilities to diagnose such dread diseases as rabies, and even produced vaccines. While I had learned something about public health and epidemiology, I was about to find that colonial veterinary medicine bore little relationship to English 'large animal practice.'

"We see all types of farm animal and a few horses," Alan had told me when I first asked to join him during vacations. "Many we see for management and husbandry advice; others for medical or surgical reasons. There are always routine calls to treat animals for parasites, de-horn calves, vaccinate the unwilling, test for tuberculosis, attend to sore feet, and treat tick borne diseases or deal with the acute problems, calving, mastitis, electrolyte imbalances and various accidents. We deal with farm animals much more individually than the farming scene in Africa."

The largest room in the headquarters of Alan Saunders's practice served several duties—front office, reception room, pharmacy and storage room for supplies. Most of the room was taken up by shelving bowed under the weight of canisters and bottles, the contents of which, at first quite bewildering, would soon become old friends. A small office opened on one side. Opposite to it a 'surgery room' served for examining small animals, dog, cats, and occasionally, pet rats or hedgehogs. There was in addition a 'sheep' room for in-house surgeries, Sheep, being easy to transport, were better operated on in the cleaner surroundings of the practice rather than in a farm barn or in a pasture.

"I bought this practice from someone who thought it time to retire," Alan said. "But without medicine and surgery he felt his life withering away. He returned to practice again on a reduced schedule. I have four men out on calls daily, including me, and two on call at night and weekends. You will always have someone to work with." He meant nights and weekends, too.

Until I started to 'see practice' I had always spent vacations working for the wherewithal to finance the rest of the school year. These vacation jobs, plus what I was about to embark on, was my true education.

4

Pulling the Wool over their Eyes

There is absolutely no substitute for a genuine lack of preparation. ~
Everything I Know I Learned in Corporate America

"Clip her up and prep her for surgery. I'll be back in a minute." Alan Saunders left me in his sheep room with a farmer and our patient while he went to answer a telephone call.

On the floor between us lay a large ewe in labor, unable to pass her lamb. I was about to assist in my first caesarian.

"Want her on the table then?" asked the farmer.

"Uh, yes," I said lamely.

Rather like the piglets, I had never been this close to an intact live sheep. My familiarity with lamb and mutton was limited to the dining table. I leaned forward to lift the poor beast on the table but the farmer reached out first. He grasped two fistfuls of wool and picked her up—nothing to it.

She lay panting on her side.

I knew Alan Saunders intended to open up her flank under a local anesthetic so the side of the ewe had to be shaved clean of wool before cleaning the surgical site. I looked for something to do the job. The farmer passed me a pair of shears. Two triangular blades joined at one end by a curved strip of metal which acted like a spring to keep the blades apart. I thought they were for clipping lawn edges, or even cutting tin.

Like my experience with the piglets, I had not

bargained for being so out of my depth. Nothing in school had prepared me for this. I was able describe the anatomy of a sheep's flank with stunning fluency, identify all the muscles on the way into the abdomen, even recite the pattern of stitches required to sew her up, or give the dose of anesthetic needed to deaden the site, but how the heck did I clip the wool?

The irony here is that the previous year we had taken one of the biggest exams in the entire course, at least one based on the greatest number of teaching hours. We had been examined in animal husbandry, the care, raising, and handling of farm animals, and I emerged an expert on sheep.

How on earth did this happen? You may well ask. By chance. While I was waiting for my turn to be summoned into the oral exam, I had picked up a farming magazine and read an article on 'in-wintering' sheep, which means keeping them indoors, in a barn, during the winter months. Saves them starving to death in the snow or on a hillside. Housing sheep poses a lot of problems which must be addressed to make it work.

Following a few mundane questions, the examiner stared at me directly and fired his best shot. "What can you tell me about in-wintering sheep?" He then sat back and examined his fingernails, or perhaps his cuticles, the modern equivalent of a woman knitting at the foot of the guillotine waiting for my head, condemned by the crime of ovine ignorance. He looked even more surprised at my answer than I did at his question. I launched into a spiffy and succinct summary of current knowledge on the subject learned assiduously about ten minutes before. I explained the use of slatted floors, the width of the slats to accommodate their tiny hooves, population density and its effect on respiratory disease, dung disposal, feeding, parasite control, heating and ventilation.

After a few minutes he cleared his throat and said we had better discuss other things. He picked up a stack of photographs to explore my familiarity with breeds of sheep. My heart sank. To me sheep were woolly beasts. With or without horns. We ate some and used others for wool, but I didn't know which. I had never been too enthusiastic about sheep, although I have always liked roast lamb with mint sauce. Lamb also goes well with red currant jelly. And of course with roast potatoes. I was about to drown.

His brow furrowed as he shuffled the pack. Then he used that stare again—this time he would stump me. "Tell me more," he said. "Tell me more about in-wintering sheep."

Our patient lay on the table. And I still had the problem of the wool.

In my left hand I took a fistful of the raw material we have used to our advantage for hundreds of years. It tented up the skin. If I tried to cut with these tin-snips I would probably make the primary incision. The farmer watched quietly.

I tried again. Same result.

"I'd better prepare the instruments," I muttered putting down the medieval tool. He grunted.

How do I deal with this mess I thought, sweat beginning to trickle down my neck. I was on the verge of running out, pleading an acute onset of twisted stomach when I was struck by an epiphany of sheer genius. "You do your own shearing?" I asked innocently.

"Yup. All three hundred of them."

"By hand?"

"Every one."

"Do you want to clear off that wool while I fetch the instruments?" I said.

It took him but a few seconds to bare the skin over the surgical site. The remaining short soft stubble was easily shaved.

The operation went fine. No one mentioned my adroit sidestep where the surgical prep was concerned. Twin lambs were safely delivered. I had survived my first close encounter with a sheep. Six or seven years later I could laugh at that surgery. By then I headed an experimental surgery unit for a research institute – devoted to sheep.

5

The Highland Fling

*Never interrupt your enemy when he is making a mistake. ~
Napoleon Bonaparte*

"Oh no, they've forgotten the floor!" I grabbed Angus Finlay's arm and pointed to the portable restraint chute, a large cage of two-inch tubular steel pipe mounted on wheels, made to hold and restrain large steers. In this case it would be used for Steven Taylor's Holstein bull.
"Aye, that's a fault with it if you're too hasty."
"But the bull..."
"Quiet laddie. The man knows what he's about, he's the farmer."
It was eight a.m. We were standing in the yard of a small Devon dairy farm in the southwest of England. Angus Finlay was a University of Edinburgh man, 1924, the former owner of Alan Saunders' practice.
His grip on my arm tightened, perhaps to stop me running to the aid of the bull. His fingers were gnarled branches growing from a square solid palm, callused and thickened from years of practicing large animal 'grunt and heave' medicine with sheep, cow, steer, and pig. His hand could engulf a 12 pound tomcat like I might hold a kitten. I noted a steely glint of triumph in this canny veterinarian's eye. I was sure mine were widening. I squirmed in his grip.
My chilled limbs tensed. This was such a new experience. I watched unsure whether I should be nervous or excited by the drama about to unfold on such a gray wet

English morning. I sensed that one shouldn't make mistakes with over a ton of scared beef.

We shivered in a light drizzle, our boots squelching in the liquid mix of mud and cow dung that coated the concrete yard outside the barn. It triggered a brief memory of squealing piglets. Farm hands tugged and heaved the crate of tubular steel pipe into position at the stall door where the bull was confined. Their breath hung heavy in the cold moist morning air. To one side a State Veterinarian stood deep in his boots scribbling on a pad of forms. He was preparing to determine whether this magnificent animal had tuberculosis. If it was positive for this dread disease, a disease communicable to humans, by law, the beast would be condemned.

The test was simple. The thickness of a fold of skin was measured. An extract of the tuberculosis germ, *tuberculin*, injected into the fold. Two days later the thickness of the skin was measured again. The amount of increase in thickness of the skin determined whether the bull was a reactor; whether it had tuberculosis, whether it would live, or die. Today the skin fold would be measured. This was the day of reckoning.

I stared fascinated at the open floor of the empty crate and glanced at the man beside me. Angus Finlay had the bored expectancy of a Roman Tribune awaiting the entrance of the gladiators and the lions.

He was a Highland Scot, square and solid like his hands, the human prototype of the off-road 4 x 4, a man not given to suffering fools gladly, and thus, as his wife Mary would aver, sometimes a little hasty of speech—which brings us to why we were there. We were standing in the yard to watch an official government man, the State Veterinarian, judge a tuberculosis *re-test* done by Angus Finlay, an official reading to see that Finlay could do it correctly because there had been a complaint against him, a complaint about his competence, about his technique—by the farmer Steven Taylor—a complaint that rankled and festered in Angus Finlay's Scottish bones. Angus knew tuberculosis!

As a State Accredited veterinarian, Angus Finlay conducted the first TB test on the bull. The result, a clear positive. The farmer was outraged. There was no way his bull had tuberculosis!

"Are you sure you did it right?" he challenged.
"Are you saying I don't know my job?"
"Positive is wrong!"
"It's no wrong!"
"My bull does not have TB!"
"Do you call me a liar?"

They had stalked around the innocent bovine beast like born-again primates, at each step growling deeper, breathing harder, hunching heads deeper into shoulders, dragging their knuckles closer to the ground. Then the farmer tossed the final insult. The test was false because of Finlay's incompetence. He would appeal; he would report; he would complain.

This was too much for the veterinarian. "Fine," said Finlay, his integrity belittled, exasperated at the farmer's attitude, seething at the injustice of the accusation and wounded by this blow to his professional pride, "If you really want your complaint to stick, you'd best tell them I, I ... You'll have to tell them I used a dirty needle."

Steven Taylor did exactly that, although he knew, as anyone who knew Finlay believed, the accusation was false.

Angus Finlay's accreditation had been immediately suspended. The judgment read in part, and I quote, "On the veterinarian's own admission he had used a contaminated needle." Finlay was still allowed to practice veterinary medicine, but not on behalf of the State.

The barn door opened and a lead rope was passed from the bull's nose ring through the bars to the front of the restraint cage. The bull followed and thrust his head through the yoke at the front, which was quickly closed and secured. Angus Finlay's hand clamped even tighter on my arm.

The bull hesitated a moment, then pushed at the bars. With no floor in the cage his feet squelched in the muck on the concrete. He moved forward. The cage moved with him, metal wheels screeching on the concrete. Clouds of steaming breath enveloped the front of the beast. The farmhand holding the rope shouted, lunged forward, slipped and let go. The bull eyed the open yard. Free of the restraint on his nose, alarmed by the cumbersome metal cage draped around his neck, the steel monster lumbered forward like a primeval tank. The front edge of the metal cage caught a fender on the State Veterinarian's car, moved the car sideways and added a deep decorator stripe to the side in passing. Alarmed by the crash and the shouts of the watchers, the animal picked up speed, accelerated across the yard, scattering farmhands like chaff.

Angus Finlay watched with a smile.

Patton could have done no better in storming the farmyard defenses. The fence collapsed before a direct frontal attack and the bull headed for the house.

"No," yelled Steven Taylor. He whipped off his jacket, ran forward, waved it in the animal's face. Terrified the beast turned through the vegetable garden, plowed a broad ragged furrow through the neat rows of young lettuce and tomatoes, uprooted a few, tore the heads off others. Then it spied the barn and, single-minded, headed back to its stall.

Alas, the cage was too wide for the opening. Door, frame and uprights were instantly reduced to splintered kindling.

From start to finish was less than two minutes.

"We'll best be getting along then," Finlay called to the State Veterinarian who stood by his car gently rubbing its new decoration. "You can call my office with the official result." He turned to me, "I mind it's time we tried Mrs. Finlay's breakfast, ye ken."

I had a fleeting thought that maybe we were leaving before the result was known because Angus Finlay didn't want to face it in case he had been wrong, followed immediately by remorse that I should doubt him. Apparently reading my mind he said, "Why, it's as clear a case as you'll ever have. You can see the reaction is positive from across the yard."

Angus told his wife about the farm visit. "Are you feeling better then, Angus?" Mrs. Finlay asked, the soul of innocence. She winked at me and set a steaming bowl of scrambled eggs on the table.

"Och, you know me, wife. I'm not a vindictive man. I do feel a wee twinge 'o guilt at not calling his attention to the missing boards, he being distracted by the re-test and about to lose his bull." He kept his gaze on the eggs, but his lips twitched as though striving not to smile. The crinklies at the edge of his eyes belied his attempt to keep a serious face. "But I didn't want to speak out too hasty again, ye ken."

6

Pig Iron

Men willingly believe what they wish. ~ Julius Caesar, William Shakespeare

"She's coming through," a startled and disbelieving farmer shouted. I felt the clutch of panic grip my bowels. Then the 300 pound Large White sow burst through a wall of straw bales, growling and squealing, an angry mother intent on doing us grievous bodily harm. She's a pig, the naïve, sophisticated part of me thought, and not known for her intelligence. Luckily my primitive mid-brain, the part nature evolved to ensure survival, took over before I had time to think this out. Mid-brain thought like primitive man facing a cave bear. Run!

We dropped what we were doing and ran, the farmer, Alan Saunders and me. This particular morning farm visit was meant to be a routine call to check a litter of piglets and inject each one with a dose of colloidal iron. They were 'Large Whites' which, when adult, would live up to their name. The iron injection was necessary because a sow's milk is low in iron. The young pigs would become anaemic if they were not allowed access to soil to root about in and supplement their diet. These piglets, born in 'farrowing crates,' and raised in pens with wooden or concrete floors, were at risk. Hence the visit. Preventive medicine, on the cutting edge of large animal practice.

The sow and her piglets were in a barn away from the other buildings, across a small field. Her temporary home, a tall, open sided building served to cover the hay and straw bales stored within. We walked across the field, the vet and the farmer chatting farm stuff, market prices, new husbandry trends, the cost of drugs.

I clumped across the field towards the barn with them, feet flopping about a bit in the boots. The farm store where I had equipped myself after a previous bout with piglets had but one size, you see, a size larger than I normally wore, but wearable.

The sow lay, all 300 pounds of her, in an ample warm pen of straw bales. We spent a few moments admiring the family. I was told that because a piglet always suckled on the same nipple, the farmer placed the smallest on the richest part of the milk bar.

The procedure was simple. The farmer lifted a piglet, passed it out to Alan Saunders and me. We inspected, poked, prodded, injected and gave it back.

The first piglet squealed at the thrust of the needle. Mom grunted. The second of her offspring squealed. She opened a tiny eye. Looked up. At number three she began to take more than a passing interest. She sat up on her haunches. We blithely continued. She grunted faster and changed her tone—querulous—a porcine "what's going on here?" We ignored her and concentrated on the piglets.

Safe behind our straw bales, we continued to catch and inject the squealing, squirming, future bacon strips.

Suddenly she stood up and squealed. She was much louder than her offspring. This caught our attention. But before we could register her intentions, she burst through the straw bales and charged. Dropping piglets, we ran. She paused briefly to sniff her abused offspring then followed our retreating persons.

An angry sow is no slouch.

Our speed accelerated.

Three humans, the acme of evolution, the top of the food chain, bacon eaters all, streaked across the field chased by a 300 pound porker.

I found pursuit-by-pig to be a startling cardiovascular exercise. Particularly in heavy rubber boots. Boots that were too large. The turf, springy in the brisk morning air on our way across the field, now presented a treacherous surface on which we strove to drive forward, our boots fighting for grip, I felt I was making no headway—like running in treacle.

She gained. We extended ourselves further.

She salivated at our heels. We scrambled through the gate. She stopped a few inches short of the fence and glared a motherly, porcine glare.

As our breathing rate lowered towards normal we stared at each other in disbelief. Suddenly we laughed. All of us except the pig. A tad hysterical, but laughter of a sort. We three elite specimens of *Homo sapiens sapiens* had blithely ignored the construction of the sow's pen. Because there was a straw barrier between Mom and us we assumed it was sturdy, and we were safe. Ha!

We tacitly agreed not to reveal our embarrassing idiocy, which is why this is the first you may have read about it. But, as it happened forty years ago, the statute of limitations has expired.

We gave the farmer a bottle of injectable iron to inject the piglets himself. I added fright to my list of emotional experiences. Cowardice is definitely the better part of valor.

***

So far I had been humiliated on my first farm visit, perplexed by my feelings castrating piglets, embarrassed at the thought of shearing a ewe, astonished at my mentor when testing a bull, and scared out of my boots by a charging pig.

Now, I would shortly receive an emotional bonus. I was about to re-visit Jonas Withins.

7

An Udder Problem

Oh what a tangled web we weave, when first we practice to deceive. ~
Sir Walter Scott.

"See you are making a fresh start. New boots are they?"

It was the pig farmer, Jonas Withins, not the one who had sprinted with us across the pasture chased by an irate 300 pound Large White sow with which I shared a bond of survival. No, unfortunately it was he of the piglet castration visit, where I had wallowed in pig dung, in what had been, at first, rather smart street clothes.

I found Withins in his barn, bent under a sick cow. An empty bottle stood on the floor. A green liquid dripped from the cow's mouth. The farmer stood from where he had been crouched underneath a large black and white Holstein cow. He eyed me up and down.

After the piglets I was always correctly dressed for farm visits, coveralls and boots. Although Alan Saunders still got a kick out of my appearance each morning. However, apart from a smile, he held his comments to himself.

Withins obviously had no intention of so doing.

My lips twitched with an attempt to answer him with a smile while ignoring his question.

"How's she doing?" I asked.

We had been called out to the farm next to Jonas Withins' to treat, or rescue, a cow fallen and stuck between two utility poles supporting a large electrical transformer.

The poles were sufficiently close together to trap the hips of a large cow.

"This will give you a chance to check up on Withins' cow with mastitis, while I deal with this one," Alan Saunders had said, grinning at me.

Mastitis is an inflammation of the udder of dairy cows, usually treated locally with antibiotics in ointment form, instilled into the teat—cows have large teats. I had serious questions about how this particular cow of farmer Withins' was being treated.

"Before you go," he called out to me. "A quick word. Withins will tell you it has *the inflammations*."

"What?"

"Inflammations."

I must have looked puzzled—I certainly felt it.

"First thing to learn, around these parts farmers recognize three conditions—the inflammations, the congestions and the mortifications. Never forget to put 'the' in front of them. They can affect any organ system—we find out later which when we examine the cow –but remember they are listed in increasing severity. The mortifications are grave."

"But how can you treat cases that way?"

"Sometimes you may have to tell a client what they want to hear, confirm the farmer's diagnosis and treat what you find. But always treat what you find in the animal honestly."

Earlier that morning Alan Saunders and I had slid, slipped, and sloshed our way through two routine farm vaccination calls, then had sneaked a brief stop at the practice to replenish supplies of inner warmth in the guise of hot tea. I had been in the largest room in the headquarters of Alan Saunders's practice, which I mentioned earlier served several duties—front office, pharmacy and storage room for supplies. Standing behind the rack of medical supplies dominating the room, the brief pause to sip the scalding hot beverage was interrupted by a familiar voice—Jonas Withins. Standing turned into hiding.

"Let me have another three bottles of your mastitis drench. Don't want to be without it."

Puzzled by the request I had peered cautiously between the bottles and boxes on the shelves. My lack of desire to see him was matched by the sudden lack of color in my face.

To the best of my knowledge there was no such medicine for mastitis. A drench is a large volume of liquid medicine forcibly poured down an animal's throat. A technique which frequently results in the giver and the *givee* both getting a large dose of the stuff—the cow inside, the farmer all over himself.

Puzzlement turned to astonishment when I saw three bottles of a sickly green liquid passed over.

When Withins had left I buttonholed Alan Saunders. "What is a mastitis drench?" I asked.

"It's a drench I use." he said, with a twinkle in his eye.

"A mastitis *drench*? What on earth is in it?"

"Oh a little turpentine oil, a few drops of brilliant green dye, dash of ethyl nitrite. Looks bad, and tastes terrible, so it must be good."

"It actually works?"

He gave an enigmatic smile. "Do you think he would have made the trip here to buy it if it didn't work?"

"But I don't see how a drench is going to help mastitis."

Before I finished with my questions the phone rang with the call to attend to the stuck cow.

Once safely cocooned in the car on the way to the cow, I pressed him again.

"The secret is how it's given," he said. "My instructions are to dilute two tablespoons in a bottle of water and give by mouth every two hours. And the farmer is told to check the teats each time to see how soon he finds an improvement. The real treatment is stripping the milk and goop from the teats. No farmer will milk an udder every two hours, so I give him an incentive—a medicine so foul looking, foul smelling, and foul tasting it must be good."

"But that's deception."

"You're right."

"Thought you had a liking for pigs?" Withins continued when he had straightened himself from under his cow.

I bravely ignored this obvious insult.

"How many doses of the mastitis drench has she had?" I asked.

"One or two."

"How's she doing?" I asked again.

Withins was too shrewd to be deterred by a stupid lame question. "Drawn to all animals are you?"

I tried to smile. My lips grimaced.

Having spent a large part of my youth in rural isolation in parts of Africa, I was always associated with animals of one species or another. I graduated from the pre-teen fascination with tame mice and reptiles, to teenage years filled with dogs and horses, various ones in need of medical and nursing care. Throw in the rehabilitation of a monkey, the rescue of a small antelope, and bumping heads with a few wilder critters, and the conditioning was complete.

I muttered a sudden fiction about growing up on a farm. Lie through your teeth, the first seeds of a budding author.

"Grow up with them then, did you?"

"We had horses mainly," I said, attempting to force a change in subject.

"Ah. Had horses, eh? They still call that farming where you were?"

I remembered reading somewhere that one did better by not resisting an opponent's strength, but adapting to it, and taking the initiative by turning it to one's own advantage. And Alan Saunders had shown me how.

"She doesn't look as bad as I thought she would," I said brightly. "I reckoned she had the congestions when you were so anxious to buy the drench."

He hesitated briefly before replying. "No," he said slowly, "Only the inflammations. I never let them get that bad."

"Alan Saunders told me you had a keen eye for your stock. Nothing much escapes you." I didn't even dare glance at him. "That's why I came to see how you managed a case of the inflammations like this. I have to learn. Do you mind if I take a look?" I bent under the cow to palpate its udder, to show him I obviously did it every day of the week.

To be truthful, I had spoken without conscious thought, guided perhaps by an unseen force.

Alan Saunders and I met later at his car.

"You were quick," I said. "The cow free already?"

"What would you have done?" said Alan.

"Me?"

"You saw her. Did you think her hips would ever fit through those poles?"

"No."

The way she laid on her chest with her legs underneath her—until the farmer had stretched them out with the ropes—it had looked obvious to me that to drag her out, either forwards or backwards, someone must cut down one of the poles. So there had been apparently no point in continuing to pull. That's why I was so surprised he had finished so soon.

"Think now. Are a cow's hips wider across, or deep?" he asked.

The cow's pelvis is angled with respect to the spine and is narrower in its depth than in its width.

"Across, I replied.

"So I turned her on her side."

Then it dawned on me. If she had been turned on her side she would have slid out with ease. I filed this away for future reference.

"About your mastitis drench," I said.

He puffed on his pipe. "*Primum non nocere*," he quoted the Latin tag, *first do no harm*. "Maybe we should consider that our first concern should be the owner."

"I don't understand."

He chuckled.

"Without an owner's confidence all our efforts in the world won't make our treatment work. If they don't believe in the treatment they seek other advice. If they don't believe in the medicine, they don't give it."

"So it works because it smells and tastes bad?"

"And because they trust us. In this case, in the words of Houdini, 'It's not the trick. It's the magician.'"

A con artist uses enough truth to give the appearance of being trustworthy, to dupe the victim. A confidence ploy and an illusion being two sides of the same coin; when is it a malicious deception, or merely a benign trick? An otherwise scrupulously honest, trusted clinician may have no qualms about using misdirection to help treat patients successfully. Like using a fictitious medicine—the mastitis drench.

When clients visit their veterinarian, without exception, they expect something to be done, or given, for their money. This sometimes complicates treatment when there is nothing wrong, so we may use a placebo. The definition in Dorland's Medical Dictionary reads--*an inactive substance or preparation, formerly given to please or gratify a patient*. In our case, gratify the owner. Now, years later, I admit to having used vitamin B12, or other vitamins, and masterful inactivity, to soothe a client. Am I taking their money under false pretences, or is such minor deception considered part of the 'whole' treatment of their pet? Certainly they feel better for it, seeing something has been done, and it allows the pet to respond to their more positive attitude.

Strangely, placebos sometimes actually work in pets when they shouldn't have any idea what is involved in their own treatment. Does it mean cures can be merely in the minds of the owners? Or does the owner give a pet enough subconscious information to change its behavior? This reasoning implies that a pet may sometimes act sick in response to its owner's actions and expressions. I'm sure they do sometimes.

I had helped deceive a farmer to convince him to treat his cow for a non-existent condition—the inflammations, with a worthless medicine—the drench, to cure a condition with a technique he wasn't aware of using—stripping the udder, because he trusted the magician. Might I be accused of trickery and deception? Conduct unbecoming a veterinary surgeon? Did the end justify the means? What would the Royal College think?

Back at the practice later in the afternoon, I was still mulling over these imponderables while we wrapped up the day.

"Oh, by the way," said Alan Saunders with a definite twinkle in his eye, "You have a new believer."

"What do you mean?" I asked.

"Jonas Withins called. He said the cow's inflammations were much better and if you were going to join the practice when you graduated, it would be fine with him if you did his farm calls. Welcome to the club. You are now a trusted magician."

Change

My first experience of small animal practice, of acting professionally as a knowledgeable veterinarian, was nurtured in the small animal clinic of the veterinary school that had tolerated me for the past umpteen years. Many of the lessons yet to be learned, and cases yet to be seen, would be etched indelibly into circuits in my brain, to stand me in good stead, or remind me of my less brilliant moments in later years. So, events which occurred during this active two year period while a house surgeon may be told when I recount incidents that really occurred much later, during my practice days, when the memories were triggered by another case.

There is a big difference between small animal practice and treating farm animals. Farmers may love their animals, but their relationship to their stock differs from that of small animals and their owners. Farmers raise animals as a business, often for food. Small animal owners, in most instances, show family bonding with their pets, and are seldom inclined to eat them. The power and meaning of the human/animal bond is taught in school nowadays. It wasn't taught half a century ago. We were left to flounder in the highly charged emotional world that united our ill patients, their worried, often terrified, owners and we clinicians. Like all professionals in clinical disciplines, we had to learn empathy tempered with emotional detachment. Without that detachment, clinicians would bear the emotional scars of every patient. Over the years, this would become a heavy burden. I read recently that one in seven veterinarians suffers burn-out within ten years of graduation.

In talking about a patient, one may also relive the emotional burden. What we express and what we really feel may be quite different. Some of us hide our true feelings behind a brusque manner, others hide behind levity.

8

A Matter of Learning

Much learning does not teach a man to have intelligence. ~ Heraclitus.

The waiting room was filled with animals clearing their throats, their bowels and their bladders. They sat, stood or lay in impossible positions on the floor, on the benches, on their owners. Here a cat hissed generic defiance at the room; there a puppy knotted its leash once more around his owner's ankles. At the end of a bench, near a window, separated from the others, a mournful Basset sat with a man old and wrinkled like himself, gently shaking his ears to a slow rhythm he alone could hear.

This was a non-profit clinic run by the veterinary school. For a nominal charge, no appointment needed, first come was first seen. So they all came early hoping to be first. Most never were. They clustered near the entrance to the examination room hoping to catch someone's attention.

Except for the old man and the Bassett.

The aroma of the clinic had a heady bouquet. It was a beautiful day. Beautiful because my veterinary diploma and license to practice were barely dry and I was still under warranty. I was, at last, practicing veterinary medicine. Wearing a traditional white coat with my badge of office, a stethoscope, around my neck, I pursued my clinical calling as the newest, most junior member of the *surgery* department, a 'house surgeon.'

I was ready for the next client.

Doc 'Magic Fingers' Malone was in charge of the clinic.

He monitored arrivals and decided which of us new men would see what case. It was a system, he said, to spread experience, to bring each new clinician along at his own pace. But I had it on good authority, from no less a worthy than my senior colleague Malcolm Bailey, a second year man, that it was Doc's assistant, 'Slippery Slim,' the chief technician, who wielded the real power. Slim it was who *actually* directed patient traffic, ultimately steered clients to examination rooms and really decided who saw what. The second year house surgeon, a man of obvious experience, had invested many a pint of good ale in Slim to learn the system.

"We don't argue about what cases we see," said the second year man. "Slim is an ex-military policeman, been here since the year dot, and those who argue with his choice of case wind up with a twelve month practice in expressing anal glands and clipping nails, and maybe cleaning ears."

My colleague assured me that pussyfooting around Slim was good training on how to relate to receptionists out in the real world. In a practice they too wield enormous power over who sees what.

I had been there a few days, but long enough that I already stood in awe of Slippery Slim. Although he was a technician he possessed remarkable clinical ability. He showed real diagnostic acumen. Sharper by far than a newly minted practitioner. He always appeared to know the patient's problem before it reached the examination room, before any one of us working in the clinic had a chance to examine it. We believed it must come from his years of experience. His knowledge, we hoped, would be a great source of help.

In the examination area I saw Slim hold open the waiting room door for the next client, scrutinize the case when it entered, murmur to the second year man, look at me, decide my fate.

So today I will examine the Basset. I literally smelled this one coming, and cleverly made a diagnosis with my nose from across the room. This was a case of ears! The characteristic odor, some folk might say a fetid cloying stench of decomposing earwax, announced the condition of moist inflammation of the ears, *otitis externa*. The stink billowed around my patient like a miasma of swamp gas.

I had dealt with a similar case earlier in the week, with great distinction I might add—perhaps not quite the same, but still inflamed ears—a case where, despite the owner's protestations that she had used nothing except the prescribed medication, I had tracked down the persistent irritation in her Poodle's ears to her habit of using a pine disinfectant, the sort associated with purifying public toilets, to clean out the crud. Undiluted. It made the ears hot, dry and brilliant red. A prescription for a bland soothing ointment to be used for a few days followed by masterful neglect—and no disinfectant—cured the problem. So, naturally, after a total of one case, I knew ears.

I greeted the Basset, learned his name was Butch, murmured banalities to the owner, cleaned, treated, prescribed, released. Beamed a winning smile. "You can pick up the medication at the pharmacy," I said, dismissing another potential success with professional aplomb.

In my ear Slim hissed, "What about its disc?"

The client waited expectantly for the result of this *sotto-voce* consult.

"No, this isn't a disc case," I said in a regretfully loud voice. "This is 'The Ears'."

"It has a disc!" Slim hissed again. "A cervical disc." He stared at me, shrugged in obvious exasperation and walked back to the waiting room—to confide in Doc Malone, no doubt.

How did Slim come up with these diagnoses? He was a technician!

He had referred to a ruptured cervical disk! That could not be overlooked. A small tear in the soft cushion of material forming a shock absorber between two vertebrae which allowed the stuffing to ooze out, press on the nerve roots, and provoke inflammation, swelling, and in the case of a disk in the neck, exquisite pain.

"Oh," I whispered. Wan smile. Palpated the neck. Dog screamed. "Need a painkiller here," I said. "Cortisone injection and rest. Help it eat off the ground, that sort of thing."

"Had one over on you, Slim did." The client said with a grin. I shrunk deeper in my shoes. "Slim knows a thing or two, he does," he added.

This client used the nickname with great familiarity. "Do you know him then?" I asked.

"Know him? Known him for years. See him down the pub all the time. He's on our darts team. You can learn a fair bit from him, I dare say."

Rub it in you old nerd, go on, rub it in.

"Of course you handled my Butch so gently you wouldn't have known how sore he was. Slim told me you would give him a painkiller, he did." He nodded to himself with grave understanding. "He knew his ears were real sore."

"A painkiller for his ears? Oh yes," I giggled. "Silly me." How stupid I have been. "Real sore," I agreed.

"Yes," the old man said. "Butch nearly bit him he did."

"Nearly bit Slim? When?"

"When he was holding him for Dr. Malone to examine out in the waiting room."

"Dr. Malone looked at Butch in the waiting room?"

"Oh yeah. Slim holds all the animals for Doc before they come in here. Not a lot slips by that man."

Which man, I thought?

"He said it was his ears?" I asked, a little puzzled.

The owner nodded with a smile. "That's all I heard Doc Malone say." He put his finger to the side of his nose to emphasize this important point. "He told Slim to give him to you."

Then I realized my client's own ageing ears did not hear with the clarity they once did. Especially when it was a confidential comment, passed quietly from the Doc to his right-hand man.

"Whispered to Slim?" I began to understand Slim's incredible clinical knowledge. And his hold over us. And I found this out without investing a single pint of ale in our chief technician.

"You're right," I said. "Thanks for the tip. I'll certainly try to learn a thing or two from someone with Slim's experience."

I put *my* finger to *my* nose like a secret Masonic sign. The old gentleman winked back at me. Butch slowly shook his head.

9

Proud Graduate

...pride, the never failing vice of fools. ~ *Alexander Pope*

Oh, how proud is a new veterinary graduate. Years of study and hundreds of gallons of beer propel a new doctor into a wealth of knowledge and debt. We emerge from school with severe deficits in sleep and money. Still wet behind the ears, ink on our diplomas not yet dry, we are about to apply this crush of learning for the betterment of the animal kingdom and our bank managers. We are ready to challenge current dogma, prove our worth and change the course of veterinary medicine, for the better, naturally.

I was no different.

Now, years later, I cringe, or laugh, at the memories of those early days, (or weeks, or months), because I have to admit, somewhat reluctantly, there was a remote chance, merely a possibility of course, of a couple of small deficits in my knowledge of a rather practical nature.

For example, I was not yet versed in the art of stroking and nurturing receptionists and technicians. But I became a quick study when I found they have a way of scheduling 'that bossy new guy' with months of expressing anal glands, cleaning chronically infected ears and dealing with all the flea allergies in the county.

I had yet to learn ways of talking to clients so they did not ask the world in general, usually in a loud voice, "Hey, how long's this one been here then?" or asking you when you were going to start vet school. And learning to understand the particular gaze dogs and cats direct at you when they are about to shred your fingers.

I had been a 'professional' but a few weeks, in a university small animal clinic. We provided our services virtually free, (we did in those days), or asked for a small donation. I saw my share of ears, fleas, limps, cuts and abrasions, and a surprising number of foreign bodies in pads. This was an inner city practice, and sidewalks are dangerous places with shards of glass, and other sharp penetrating objects.

I was on clinic duty one morning, a Monday, the usual confused and busy start to the week which always collected the accumulated disorders and accidents of a weekend. The Setter limped in at his handler's side, still happy to see anyone. He was an intact male, about seven or eight years old. Good physical condition. But lame. He had been found several days before, running free in a local park and taken to the animal shelter where it was noticed the poor dog was limping. No collar. No identification. When the lameness didn't resolve after a few days, the shelter staff sent him to us for examination.

There was a swelling below the elbow, obvious to an astute new graduate highly trained in observation, clearly visible from where I stood behind the examination table.

The introductions complete, I examined the dog. The swelling on its forearm was quite firm. Clinical alarm bells rang somewhere in my subconscious. A swelling, in that location, in a middle-aged large breed dog was highly suspicious for an *osteosarcoma*, a highly malignant bone tumor. It is the sort of suspicion one hates.

"Now then," I said in the calm and confident manner of my meager experience. "I think we should X-ray his leg."

I made the arrangements for X-rays and saw a couple of other cases before the results arrived. The bone had the classic appearance of a malignancy. I counted off the significant changes in the appearance of the bone. Loss of parts of the outer wall of the bone, areas where the bone was thinner, areas of new bone standing erect like a palisade fence, lines of bone radiating out from the swelling like a starburst. The sort of diagnosis one hates when it comes out of the blue. The animal had looked fine when found in the park, except for a slight limp. Now I was about to diagnose a terminal condition. In an unclaimed shelter dog there was little option but euthanasia.

Torn between pride at such a swift and accurate diagnosis, and sadness that such an attractive, friendly and otherwise healthy dog had an active cancer I carried out the shelter's wishes and sent the body to the path lab for an autopsy.

The result came through in due course. I seized it eagerly, anxious to have confirmation of my diagnostic acumen and skills. It was not quite what I had imagined. A terse note was appended from the pathologist. "Please do a *thorough* physical examination on your cases in future."

This malignancy was not a primary bone tumor. It was a *metastasis*, one that had spread from a cancer of the tonsil!

I was suitably crushed. I had taken a shortcut to a brilliant diagnosis, so I thought. And I had screwed up. Hah! I was yet to learn such humbling moments would be repeated, in other ways, over the years.

Despite my mistaken diagnosis, I took solace from the fact that euthanasia had been the appropriate action.

Fortunately my next case appeared to be routine; a lady with a small pug. The present owner had owned her barely a week, a six-year-old reject from a breeding colony, when she made the mistake of setting her dog down—despite prominent warning notices against such behavior—on an escalator. Dogs do not know about the transition from moving staircase to solid floor. They know even less about reading the warning notices cautioning against such behavior.

The little dog's left hind foot had been caught in the metal 'comb' at the end of the moving, folding, metal steps. It had been damaged almost beyond recognition. Two toes were missing. The others were partially skinned.

I examined the mess. There was little hope of doing a primary repair. There was not enough skin to cover the wounds. The little dog would have to endure frequent bandage changes while her foot healed slowly.

I changed the bandage every other day. I think it was on their third clinic appointment when the owner complained that she did not want to continue this protracted treatment with its frequent visits and, so would I please put her to sleep.

This was my first experience of dealing with owner convenience. This was not a problem with payment or charges, we charged nothing. We did ask the owner to make a contribution to their pet's care if they could afford it. This owner resented spending the time to help the pet whose injury she had been responsible for in the first place. But unlike the Setter, this was a perfectly treatable case.

I consulted Doc Malone. We were of the same mind. We should not put the pet to sleep for convenience. However we differed in the solution.

"You need a pet," he said. "She is small. She would be a perfect fit in your flat."

Seeing my surprised stare he added "Take her!"

There is not much call for dogs with an odd number of feet and few potential owners, except for softies—but I believe the measure of a man is whether he can admit to being a softy and still hold high his head. I adopted her. I named her Dammit.

I had not counted on the reaction of my fiancé to my careful and deliberate decision, a reaction best illustrated by recounting an incident that happened years later in upstate New York.

10

Pygmy Cabbages

Cabbage: A vegetable about as big and as wise as a man's head. ~
Ambrose Bierce

The day stretched time.

Morning office hours over, surgical list complete, we retreated deep into our clinical castle behind an upstate New York winter moat of ice and snow. Such time could not be wasted. The urge to clean motivated clinician and nurse alike. Gripped in a paroxysm of busy work, we vied with each other to see who could be first to organize and change the drugs from alphabetic storage to functional groups like antibiotics, and miscellaneous, or wash the coffee pot. This was truly the creative art of moving heaps and cupboard stuffing.

A walk-in rudely interrupted our routine. Dragged by a large hairy snow-covered dog, a man lurched through the door.

"His ear's been swollen like this for five days, doctor," the owner said.

The left earflap was noticeably swollen. It hung from the side of his head, pulling at it, trying to twist the neck sideways. Every few seconds the dog gave a weak shake of the head, banging the offending ear against his cheek.

In the clinical record I made a note in technical jargon, *aural hematoma*. "It's a large blood blister," I said. "Caused by shaking his head. He's ruptured a small blood vessel. I'm afraid he needs surgery to repair the ear flap."

"What happens if it is left alone?" the owner asked.

"Unfortunately the ear will crumple," I said. "It will look like...like a..." Usually cleverly articulate, I was at a loss for the right word. My mind was blank. What was I trying to say?

I knew what a crumpled ear would look like but the words were in limbo somewhere between conception and speech.

"Like a pygmy cabbage," I mumbled.

"A pygmy cabbage?"

"All crumpled."

"You mean a Brussels Sprout."

I sighed. It had happened to me again, *anomia*, a partial forgetfulness, a selective amnesia for words, due, it is said in the learned books, to a lesion in Wernicke's and/or Broca's speech areas of the brain. Possibly due, it is said in the learned books, to severe psychological stress. The learned books are fond of naming parts of the body after people—they do it with highways and bridges now—where was I? Ah yes, I remember. (The learned books have not given a name to the area where memory resides, probably because no one remembers where it is.)

Before I could add anything coherent to the conversation with the client, I flashed back to my early clinical days, a time in the mid-sixties. The ink on my diploma was still wet, but fresh from long nights of learning, with rare and unusual clinical answers burned into memory awaiting instant recall, I was prepared, like Don Quixote, to battle the specters of disease and trauma with the marvels of medicine and surgical repair.

We were sitting at a table in the communal kitchen in my girlfriend, Gillian's 'digs.' She had her own room, but shared the kitchen and bathroom with several other tenants. The house was full of rooms, each one its own universe, whose occupants, separated in their private worlds, met occasionally on the staircase, the communal kitchen, or at a locked bathroom door. We sat, the two of us, arguing about the dog. The dog I had recently adopted.

"It can sit in a soup plate?" she said, eyes bugging. "I don't want a runt, I want a big dog."

"The size of a dog is in inverse proportion to the self esteem of its owner," I snapped. But, now was not the time to discuss her insecurities. Instead I sprung niftily onto my high horse. "I'm helping this dog," I said. "If I don't take her, she will be put to sleep."

"It's a she?"

"She's a she."

"You don't have to make it your problem."

"What do you think I went to Vet School for?"

Really, the intimate details of our spat will simply bore you. It droned on like a mediocre tennis game. Back and forth, back and forth. Insult and barb, volley and lob. Deuce—advantage me. Deuce—advantage her. We stared at the table and thought up new arguments, new barbs and new insults. This could be considered 'domestic practice'—Gillian and I intended to marry in three months—yes, to each other. Our world shrunk to expressive mouths and eyes.

I had named the little dog Dammit.

So, here we were in the communal kitchen, my fiancée and I, and the spirit of Dammit.

Unknown to us, in a universe parallel to our own, one that shared this kitchen, another domestic couple was cooking. Their food was on the stove. It had been there a while. We didn't know. They were from the second floor. Foreign. Man and wife heard our heated, steamy language blistering the paint on the closed kitchen door. Loath to intrude on us they waited on the stairs until our argument came down to a mere simmer. And waited, and waited.

Finally they came in. We looked up at their entrance. And noticed for the first time a thick-layered cloud of smoke hanging above our heads clear up to the ceiling. The bottom rippled and undulated with dark sensual waves that lapped at the walls. It was their dinner going up in smoke, pouring thick, black and acrid, from a pot on the stove. It pushed upwards, a fat coiling column, flattened against the once white ceiling, pushed the lower layers lower still, to the undulating waves.

We were embarrassed and horrified. How could we sit there and not notice? But we hadn't noticed. They didn't believe we hadn't noticed. Really, we hadn't noticed.

Plunged in the water-filled sink the pot sizzled and bubbled like a volcanic mud-hole. We peered in its depths. A black porous mass coated the bottom like solidified lava.

"What was it?" I asked.

"You know, those little..." He couldn't place the name—he was foreign. "Those things like little cabbages. Pygmy cabbages," he said.

"Brussels sprouts," I said.

"Yes. Brussels sprouts."

They stared at us accusingly. We opened the windows to the raw March evening air. Better pneumonia than asphyxiation. We muttered apologies. They glared. We left in silence.

I was appalled at our lack of consideration. They were appalled at our lack of consideration. Burnt offering. Incinerated pygmy cabbages.

Our own practice domestic spat forgotten for the time being we went out, boarded a bus for the movies to see Michael Cain in The Ipcress File—*Induction of Psychoneurosis by the Chronic Repetition of Stress*, like vet school.

I came back to the present.

The walk-in client smiled. Feebly. I felt his doubts wash over me. If I can't describe his dog's problem how could I possibly deal with it?

"I like cabbages," he said. He left with his dog.

Darn. And I've even been to Brussels—Brussels, Belgium that is. I could say it. And I ate sprouts, bean, alfalfa, bamboo, others. But I couldn't put them together. My speech synthesizing circuits had developed a glitch.

Somewhere in Broca's or the other fellow's area whose name I forgot, I had developed a *stretched synapse*, a *damaged dendrite*, an *anomalous axon*, or perhaps merely a common nerve cell, a *neuron*, crumpled and burned by that trial domestic spat. Like an overcooked pygmy cabbage.

***

Postscript: When they met, the bond between my fiancé and Dammit was instantaneous and complete.

11

Dammit Takes Tea

My feast of joy is but a dish of pain. ~ Chidiock Tichborne

Like their owners and their veterinarians, some dogs know when to stop eating and some don't. I was about to learn that Pugs, well this particular model, the little newcomer in my household, had no self-control. Being still naïve, I decided one evening to see if she had a limit switch to her appetite. After she had finished her measured amount of food, I added some left-over steak, a few slices of bread, and was about to give her more scroungings from the kitchen when my newly minted wife spotted me. Before you exclaim, I should add that, like most sensible men, I have had the good fortune to choose women much more sensible than I with whom to share my life.

"Stop that! You'll make her poop all over the place."

It took Gillian much longer to explain to me why I was wasting what meager education I had received about dogs, and that I could clean up after my over-indulged pooch in the morning. I also learned that ownership of our new pet was labile—when loveable, she was claimed by my wife—when all was not well on the canine front, she became mine.

Unfortunately there were three floors between our flat and Dammit's bathroom, a meager grass strip alongside the car parking space outside the clinic. Luckily our hallway, Dammit's preferred doggie bathroom for that night— her legs were too short to reach the grass doggy pooping-platz in time—had no carpet. Gillian was, of course, quite right about the intestinal hurry-up caused by overeating. Because she had not invested her life savings in specialized courses to learn this—something she reminded me of on occasion—I added the experience to the mental file that held stupid questions of sheep husbandry and piglet castration. The clean-up, particularly the aroma in the poorly the ventilated hallway, brought back vivid olfactory memories of being soaked in piglet poop.

As I may have mentioned before, there were two interns, or Assistant Lecturers in Surgery if one wants to sound posh, Malcolm Bailey, the second year man, and me. As a reward for being on duty every other night and every other weekend, we were each given a rent-free flat on the top floor of the building. Slippery Slim lived in a third apartment. The landing at the top of the stairs leading to the flats also opened onto a flat roofed area. This could be reached by climbing two steps and squeezing through a small door. Gillian liked to use the roof garden. One afternoon she carried a tray of the necessary fixings for British afternoon tea to her favorite hangout. As she stood on the top step, balancing the tray on one hand while she fumbled with the door latch, our little bundle of snuffles bounded up the steps, hit the tray with her head and knocked over a pint milk bottle. The falling bottle landed firmly on Dammit, smacking the dog's head against the step before shattering in a shower of milk and glass on the floor. Now it was Gillian's turn to clean up a mess. A pint of milk spreads a long way. Dammit made herself scarce until the afternoon tea ceremony was resumed, then she launched herself at the steps once again and joined my wife on the roof.

I fed her as usual that evening (a portion controlled meal). Unlike her normal behavior, she took her time to eat. She trotted back and forth from her feeding spot to the sitting room, taking a good two minutes to finish her delicious dinner.

"Are you going to look at her?" I was asked by 'you-know-who.' I agreed this uncommon behavior warranted investigation.

The search for the cause of her delayed food-wolfing-down event was not hard to diagnose. The abrupt meeting between the milk bottle and the step had broken her jaw. However, she still hadn't left a morsel of food on her plate.

An X-ray showed that the edges of the fracture were not badly displaced. By taping the jaws together, loosely enough to allow her to lap and pant, and feeding a semi-liquid diet for a few weeks, she was restored to a picture of gluttonous health. However, despite the skill and care I had lavished on Dammit following the tea-break—an accident never again discussed in polite circles—my feeding practices did not recover from the pooping episode. From then Gillian joined Dammit to watch me measure the food portion when my hungry little dog waited impatiently for her dinner. Looking on the positive side, I had at least earned a measure of attention from both the gentler members of our ménage—more than can be said for many husbands.

12

That's Life

So as long as you're stepping in it, show it some respect.

"And where, I might ask, do you think you're going?"

An early Darth Vader look-alike, representing the law, stepped quietly from the shadows and planted his number fifteen boots firmly on the sidewalk in front of the suspect.

Mike sighed. The possibility of being stopped always existed, he knew that, but it had been a gamble he was prepared to take. His mother was relying on him.

English policemen are invariably polite—or they used to be—even when confronted with a suspicious personage at three in the morning, a potential villain, walking in the vicinity of King's Cross railway station in London, carrying a swag bag.

Fifty years ago, this area of London, not far from the veterinary college, was a place one might choose to avoid at night, particularly walking alone, unless one really had to, or one had a predatory nature. The road led past railroad bridges supported on huge brick arches where once hundreds of horses were stabled during the almost forgotten equine era, before the internal combustion engine became the terror of the highways. In the dark, it could be forbidding.

"Home," Mike replied. "I was working at the Veterinary College."

This was obviously a sound reason to be there, as any normal person would understand, even if the normal person were a policeman, and a doubting Thomas to boot—size fifteen.

"At three in the morning?"

"I was working late."

"So you were indeed! And what might we have in the bag?"

One can't, or shouldn't, argue with a copper.

"Elephant sh-t," said Mike believing that by telling the truth, he wouldn't have to struggle to compose and remember a fiction—a lie that is.

There is a magic about elephant scat that the policeman did not appreciate, since he didn't come across many elephants, or their deposits, in London. Fresh elephant scat stinks. Believe me. But there are some to whom a pile of pachyderm scat tells a story although they are not usually policemen. I once knew such a man. His name was Jan van der Merwe. He was fascinated by elephant dung.

Growing up in Tanzania on the east coast of Africa, (at that time known as Tanganyika), while it was still a British colony, provided an educational experience that differed in content from the usual curriculum found in inner London. This was before the 'Winds of Change' cleared the air and ushered in the current changes and colors on world maps. My father's work involved nursing buses and trucks on cross country routes for the railways, mainly on dirt and wash-board roads, where 'mechanical' trouble preyed on unwary drivers.

One safari, scheduled to last longer than usual, provided an opportunity for my mother and I to go with him. We stayed with the van der Merwes, a South African family, at Itigi, a tiny rail stop on the central railway line. Here locomotives stopped to refresh supplies of coal and water. The area was surrounded by savannah, 105 miles from the present capital, Dodoma. Now, sixty years later, the population has grown to about 1000 people. In addition to the railway station, the town boasts a post office, a hospital and a well.

I believe Mr. van der Merwe worked for the railway too, but, in addition, he acted as the local large-animal game-control officer. If a village had a hippo problem he dispatched himself to deal with it. The problem might be an elephant raiding the *shambas* (farms), or a lion preying on cows. And he shot game so we had meat to eat, the sanitary facilities at the local butcher being somewhat sparse. He also rescued orphan animals which then had the free run of the house and surroundings.

There were three little van der Merwes. Together we squandered our time playing with orphan bush pigs and antelopes, usually followed everywhere by ducks and young guinea fowl eager to join in. When we bored of those games, we chased lizards and skinks, caught grasshoppers to feed to chameleons, or moved them from place to place to watch them change color. Many evenings, both families piled in a car to drive around the savannah, animal watching or hunting. And one day we decided to have a picnic.

Our Ford station wagon was commandeered for the picnic. My father drove, while Jan van der Merwe sat in the passenger seat with the door slightly open, holding a rifle cradled in the crook of his elbow. His wife sat between them. Mum sat with all us kids in the back seat. There were more guns stored behind us.

The area is best known for a type of bush growth known as the 'Itigi-Sumbu Thicket,' quite different from the surrounding woodland and savannah grassland. This area of vegetation, some miles from the village, is unique. Branches of the thorn bushes intertwine to form a canopy so dense that almost no light reaches the ground.

A person can scarcely penetrate it, except perhaps by belly-crawling through the carpet of fallen thorns. However elephants can force their way through the dense thickets, leaving a track that is hard to see as the vegetation springs back towards its original position.

We drove down a narrow track between this high thorn-scrub to reach our picnic spot. The wheels in the dirt ruts, either side of a narrow strip of brown grass, churned the dust into a dense ochre cloud that blotted out our passage. The thick tall bushes were so close they whipped past in a blur. The longer branches scraped the sides of the car. It felt like we were flying, but we were barely going fifteen or twenty miles an hour.

Ahead in the middle of the track we saw elephant droppings and large footprints in the dust, longer than they were wide, where the beast slid forward with each stride. It must have been a big one; there were only two prints on the track.

Jan wouldn't let anyone near it until he made sure the rightful owner wasn't around to argue about our interest. He stared at the deposit, walked around it, crumbled it in his fingers (right there, in the bush, where there were no washrooms), smelled it, and from the temperature, texture, and aroma that swirled and eddied in almost visible waves, determined it had been some time since Jumbo passed.

Eventually, I moved close enough to smell it, although not with degree of enthusiasm that Mr. van der Merwe expected.

On either side of the road there was a difference in the scrub. To the right the branches pushed into the track. To the left they were pushed away as if some giant body had crushed them in passing. It had. I was about to follow when Mr. van der Merwe grabbed my arm. "Never follow a big animal into thorn scrub like that. You'll never get back."

I looked at the branches, the long thorns. All were bent the same way—away from me.

"You can follow easily," he said, "but when you turn round, all those branches will point toward you. You won't be able to move."

Mike had found his elephant scat in a quite different way. He was an anatomy technician at the veterinary college a scant half mile from the station. An elephant had died in the city that day, probably in a zoo. The details escape me, but I do know that the carcass had been promptly sent to the veterinary college for its skeleton to be cleaned and mounted. For an anatomy technician, such opportunities were few and far between. On the day of its delivery, Mike grabbed at the chance. He called his mother to tell her he might well be home late. Her disappointment was tempered by her delight at the enormous amount of organic fertilizer Mike promised for her roses.

And so it happened that late that night, or early the next morning depending on your point of view—anyway, about 3 am—Mike was confronted by the owner of the size fifteen boots who demanded to know what he carried in the bag.

"Elephant sh-t," Mike had replied—remember, I told you that.

"A pink one I trust," replied the law.

"No, a regular grey one."

"Don't you start any funny stuff with me, young man. Open it up."

"Really it's elephant sh-t. You sure you want me to open it?"

The policeman stood firm

Mike opened the bag. He anticipated the ripe aroma; he had worked with it all day. To his credit the policeman did not void his own stomach contents in the road. He did glare, so Mike said, but, British to the core, his upper lip remained stiff. And of course he couldn't lose face now, could he?

The record does not show what Mike's mother's neighbors thought of her organic gardening gift. I expect they probably had a similar response as the policemen. But the French have an expression that covers both situations, *c'est la vie*, which means 'that's life.' It can also be translated into English as 'oh well, sh-t happens.'

13

Bare Skin

Many a dangerous temptation comes to us in fine gay colors that are but skin deep. ~ Mathew Henry

Not long after Dammit entered my life, and before Gillian, my fiancé, and I knotted our lives in a twist, or vice versa, fate stepped into the relationship between me and Slippery Slim, the head technician at the clinic.

What had been a typical hum-drum morning brightened when Slim led the 'client' to my examination table. "She needs to see *you*," he said with a raised eyebrow.

A young lady, well made up, her hair piled in a beehive, a popular fashion of the time, picked up a small white poodle she had in tow and put him on the examination table.

"Hello, Mabel," I said. Slim's other eyebrow jumped up to join its colleague.

As she bent over, a skimpy uniform, clearly visible under her gaping raincoat, proclaimed the fact that she was employed in the personal entertainment industry.

"How's he doing?" I asked, quite ignoring Slim who hovered, eyebrows dancing, as if reluctant to leave.

"He's fine now. Thanks. Look at him." She turned her dog this way and that.

I remembered the case clearly, a mild skin problem. I had not forgotten the client either.

"He looks absolutely cured," I said. I examined the rest of her poodle for the sake of appearances, you understand,

and to further perplex Slippery Slim, who continued to hover in apparent 'undecided' mode.

Mabel smiled at me and gave me an envelope. "My boss asked me to give you this, as a sort of thank you. She's awfully grateful. Oh, and she said to drop by anytime, if, you know, you want to examine any of the other dogs, or need to relax. The address is in the envelope. Ta-ta." She twirled on a stiletto heel and headed to the door.

Slim opened and closed his mouth soundlessly several times, the appearance of the 'lady' having empowered a unique force to seize his vocal cords.

"She's one of our clients," I said. "I treated her dog."

A little background is in order.

With the introduction of new vice laws in Britain aimed at curbing public solicitation by the world's oldest profession, loitering, with intent to do you-know-what, became a punishable offence. Not to be out-done, the enterprising ladies acquired small dogs. When accosted by a stalwart minion of the law for the aforementioned crime, they claimed merely to be walking their dogs.

Once dogs were introduced into the business equation it was inevitable that our professions, the oldest and one of the newest, would bump heads.

She had brought her dog in for an emergency consultation on a day when our managing technician, Slim, was away. Her unfortunate canine partner had developed a minor skin problem—the cause is irrelevant. However, she had had it treated at the 'Elsewhere' clinic. They had wanted to shave the poor dog. When she declined treatment that would have 'made all his skin bare,' they gave her a bright yellow ointment to treat the lesions.

She intimated that her business had, as a consequence, suffered a setback. Yellow blotches indicating an obvious skin disease are no better as an advertisement than patches of bare skin in a line of work where appearance is all, including the appearance of her walking partner.

I remember giving her something, a cream or ointment,

to remove the offending medication. It had worked. All traces of the yellow color had gone.

I waited until Slim was out of sight before opening the envelope. It held two crisp pound notes and a brief letter, on perfumed notepaper, re-stating the invitation to visit the home establishment anytime I was in the area. Bartering was mentioned. Perhaps she thought she had found a consultant for her kennel—or would it be a stable? I forget the proper collective noun for such a group of ladies, or their pets.

Slim never mentioned the young lady episode to me. Of course, Dr. Malone knew about her initial visit—after all he had steered her to me in the first place, because as I explained earlier, he encouraged our education, each at his own pace, even though I was not sure what I had been meant to learn from this particular client—oops, case. Perhaps he had told Slim. However, even Doc didn't know about the envelope with its reward, the written invitation, or the offer to barter services.

Slim's demeanor the rest of the day suggested that I had risen in his social scale. Either that, or he could not believe what he had seen. I think he was jealous, although the green tinge to his skin may have been due to the fluorescent light in the clinic. However, sensing my changed standing with him, I could afford to be generous. That night, I saw Slim in the pub. I had left Dammit, my little Pug, at home but Slim had his Jack Russell terrier with him. Flush with my well-earned gratuity I bought him a beer. We lived in flats next door to one another so together we walked home, down the street, with his dog.

∗∗

Following my role as a house surgeon I spent the next ten years in academia 'on both sides of the pond' before reprising a clinical position in surgery to re-orient myself to clinical practice. When I moved away from London, I left behind physical evidence of another memory from my student days.

14

A Worm of a Different Scale

Il nous faut de l'audace, encore de l'audace, toujours de l'audace. (We must dare, and dare again, and go on daring.) ~ *Georges Jacques Danton*

The small crocodile, comfortably confined on my knee, maintained a private *cordon-sanitaire* around my rush hour seat on the London underground. The damp and odor of the bleak November fog clung to the close press of rush hour bodies. In this standing-room-only world, I had a seat to myself. Even the seats on either side of me were empty. Now and again there was movement in the box I carried, clearly reminding all concerned that inside was something live!

Close standing passengers, stoic in their impassivity, glanced at me with obvious concern, but, true to their stiff upper lips, kept a tight rein on their thoughts and made no comment. We were all still quite British fifty years ago.

A telegram had arrived at 2:00 pm: *Prepare receive live crocodile arriving Heathrow 10.30 a.m. stop Dad.* Heathrow, London's major airport, lay 20 miles distant, right across the city.

This incident, reaching out to haunt the fall of my junior year, reminded me of the idiocy of the previous summer. During this pause before my junior year, the last before I would spend summer vacations seeing practice, I visited the parental home in Malawi—that's in Africa, east-central, down a bit from Tanzania, in a bit from

Mozambique—where I lived during my teenage years.

At some time during the home visit I was invited by two older persons, skilled in bush craft and the ways of wild creatures, one a professional safari guide no less, to join them in 'sport-fishing'. Our quarry was Tiger fish in the Shire River. My parents, by this time quite eager for me to do something other than reorganize their lives, urged me to go. "Wonderful opportunity. See Africa in the raw. Splendid man, that guide—professional you know—couldn't do better," and other parental platitudes.

We sailed boldly where no aluminum outboard had dared before—cleverly dodged huge islands of vegetation floating on the river, swollen by recent rain, which threatened to swamp our small craft. We bravely fended off overwhelming attacks of ravenous mosquitoes scavenging for human blood. We cast expertly for vicious Tiger fish. We sweated. We burned in the sun. We dehydrated.

We took no fish.

Then the motor quit.

Our paddles flew in a frantic effort to reach the nearest bank, racing against current, floating islands and possible wild critters of the deep. At the edge of the river, branches and roots grew from the water forming a dense barrier between the boat and dry land. Our desperate hands grabbed the branches and pulled the craft into their protection. They were our hands. Draped in a heavy blanket of river scented air, gorged mosquitoes floundered and drowned in the bilge. Less blood-thirsty insects shrilled a sharp descant to the chorus of birds chirping, twittering and cawing through the air. Our sweaty bodies waited for rescue.

In contrast to our jungle, the vegetation on the far side of the river was scrub bush and grass. It belonged to a different country, Mozambique. The sandy river bank lay exposed and undercut by the recent high water. Things moved in the grass. Small shiny animals scurried forward and dived into the river several feet below. We heard the plop, plop of their bodies entering the water, and harsh shrill cries. In silence we witnessed the first swim of young crocodiles, newly hatched, maybe six inches long, fingerlings of the crocodilian world.

Hours later, ignominiously towed home behind a two man dugout canoe, much of our blood remained behind as testimony to our visit in the bloated bodies of so many, once flying, insects. The baby crocs we left to their new world.

Next day, boat engine repaired, my hosts were eager to return to view the hatchlings. After straying across the watery border into Mozambique, sans passports, visas or sundry immigration officials, we found the reptilian nest. It lay some way from the bank. Fortunately for the crocodiles it held simply empty shells. In the calm water close to the bank, only their eyes and nostrils visible, we saw the miniature reptiles. They floated absolutely still, bodies hanging below the surface. At our slightest movement they submerged, sinking away from danger. We kept out a wary eye for Mom. Her teeth were bigger than her babies.

Professional though he was, while my new-found guide gloated about the money to be made selling these innocents to zoos throughout the world, he had no more success in catching these tiny baby crocodiles than he did fishing for Tiger fish.

In late August I returned to London, to the relief of the wild animal word, without any trophies, looking forward to the first semester of my junior year. Meanwhile back at the ranch unseen forces were at work. Sometime in September a crocodile arrived like a foundling on my parent's doorstep. In keeping with the classical history of such abandoned waifs and strays, it bore a note. 'Better late than never. Sorry we didn't catch one in the summer.' My fishing host had remembered me.

As the story went, and need I remind you of the twists and turns of family tales, the new arrival kept scrabbling out of the bathtub. It claimed fingers for its own. Screamed at the dog—young crocodiles can make a terrible noise—then parental inspiration followed their exasperation at the discourteous guest –"Our son can use it. He's going to be a vet' nary. He'll know what to do." So the little monster joined the jet set.

Back to that gray November afternoon.

The telegram had jolted me, but my inquiry to Heathrow airport about the package was met with stony indifference. "Do you know how many parcels arrive here daily?"

I mentioned that my parcel contained a live crocodile. Within minutes it was located, and I faced a barrage of questions. "Should it be fed? Walked? Taken to the R.S.P.C.A.? See a vet? Have shots?"

My concerns were elsewhere. "Uh. How big is the parcel?" I asked, imagination in overdrive. I had visions of a crate, ten feet long, weighing half a ton. Men with ropes. Cranes.

"'Bout three feet one way I should say. Yeah, 'bout that. By 'bout six by six."

"Feet?" Oh my God!

"Not feet. Inches. That do yer? There's a lot 'o holes in it."

Holes? My imagination was still in overdrive. Were those self-inflicted or for air? Guess I would soon find out.

"What about an import license?" I asked.

"Can't say 'bout that. Board 'o Trade 'ave to help you with that one."

"Board of Trade? I have this crocodile at London Airport..."

A voice identical to one I later heard introducing the Hallmark Hall of Fame replied—a voice to make William Buckley sound coarse. The voice also laughed like a basso-profundo whooping crane. "License? Only if you're going to make it into handbags, what? Who-ah, who-ah, who-ah!"

Riding the underground to the airport was uneventful.

So was collecting the parcel, except there had to be a Doubting Thomas ready to put his fingers in the holes. I believe he still has all his digits. I rode back in my personal *cordon-sanitaire*, profusely labeled parcel on knee: Beware, Dangerous, Live Crocodile, Do NOT Put Fingers in Holes, Rush.

My concern was how to get it out of the box. Being fundamentally a coward, I took the line of least resistance.

"Regent's Park Zoo Reptile house. Keeper speaking."

"Ah yes. I have this crocodile."

The keeper opened the box, lifted out a cloth flour sack, untied the neck and emptied the contents onto the tiled floor. A two and a half foot crocodile tried to do wheelies on the slippery surface. Casually, the keeper bent down, caught the tail, grasped the poor baby behind the head and lifted it up.

"Donating it to the zoo then, are you?" he asked. "Can't put it on display though."

I raised my eyebrows. After all, I was beginning to feel more confident. I was now a Regent's Park Zoological Garden Patron.

"See, the problem is someone recently gave one to Prince Andrew, so his is on show. Drawing quite a crowd too he is. Still, we can keep yours as an understudy, 'bout the same size they are. If we need him, no-one will ever know the difference."

The Zoological Society sent me a certificate thanking me for the donation of one *Crocodylio niloticus*, genus Crocodylus, from the Latin *crocodilus*, from the earlier Greek *krokodilos*, 'worm of the pebbles' named after its habit of basking in the sun. With patronage came the privilege to visit the zoo freely. So one afternoon I slipped into the reptile house, through the door marked private, into the corridor running behind the display cages. I, who had so recently braved the rigors and hazards of the African bush, found a large Mississippi alligator blocking the way.

Fortunately it was facing the other way so I did not have to stare him down. Even so, this intrepid hunter froze. I awaited his next move. Hopefully it would be away from me.

"He's 'armless," the keeper said poker faced. "Want to pat him then?" He was calling my hand when I wanted to beat a hasty retreat. I didn't fancy being an alligator's dinner.

Prince Andrew never heard about the little drama when I visited his pet's understudy, but some years later he played out his own drama in the Falkland Islands flying a helicopter, where he called Argentinean hands, as he played target for Exocet missiles, daring them to attack him, slipping out of their line of flight at the last second, maintaining a British *cordon sanitaire* in the waters off the Argentinean coast. Which was rather more dangerous than patting a somnolent alligator on the behind on a quiet afternoon.

By chance, in 1986, I was in London again, at the time of Prince Andrew's wedding to Fergie. He still dared to play dangerous games. And in 1992 I returned from yet another trip to London to hear, that like my meeting with the Mississippi alligator, he had beaten a strategic retreat from a marriage on the rocks.

And I was left to wonder; my *Crocodilio niloticus* was now too big to carry on my knee, but did it still play understudy?

And is the royal croc yet on display?

Interlude

In 1966, whilst a house surgeon, I was asked to assist a heart surgeon in anesthetizing dogs to develop a procedure for heart-lung transplants. This I did, and felt flattered, when after a while, I was asked to join the team.

Here was an opportunity to work with Donald Ross, the most prominent British heart surgeon and Donald Longmore, one of the most prominent cardiac physiologists in the country. Serious consideration however showed how idiotic this would be. I would, like a follower of Moses, wander forever in an intellectual wilderness, lost in the great knowledge divide separating us.

However the power of their discussions spurred my interest in applied physiology. I wrote to the governing body of Anesthesia in the UK asking if I was qualified for, and would be permitted to attend any of their courses. To my surprise, not only was I invited to attend post graduate courses by the Faculty of Anaesthetists of the Royal College of Surgeons, I was welcomed as the first veterinarian to do so.

When, in 1966, a faculty position in anesthesia was advertised at another Veterinary school, I had an edge. "If we offered you a faculty position," I was asked, "would you mind terribly spending time in the local medical school studying the anesthesia residency didactic courses with practical exposure in three teaching hospitals?" I may have hesitated a second or two before accepting.

Flushed with pride at my appointment, I soon came close to a premature end, or what the stars would call, 'an inauspicious start' to a career.

15

The Break

If there is a 50-50 chance that something can go wrong, then nine times out of ten it will. ~ Paul Harvey

"Okay. I've got him," the surgery technician said. He was holding a young stallion firmly by the halter rope. I moved to the horse's side, pressed my left hand into the side of its neck to raise the jugular vein, swabbed it with alcohol soaked cotton and injected a small bleb of local anesthetic into the skin over the vein.

We were standing on a large padded rubber mat in the veterinary school's large animal surgery. The horse in question, a young thoroughbred, was being readied for surgery. Half an hour before it had been given an intramuscular injection of tranquilizer. Now it was time to administer an anesthetic.

There was not a great deal of the horse one could see. Body and head were hidden by a sturdy padded blanket held in place by leather straps. The metal shoes had been removed, and all four legs wrapped in protective boots. With the addition of an ornate saddle, this horse would have passed for a medieval steed ready for the jousting tournament. The man at its head, the one who 'had got him' had been at the job for 20 years. There was not an animal been through the department that he had not handled.

As a newly minted graduate, recently appointed to the

surgical staff, this would be my first solo anesthetic procedure in a horse. However I had assisted with several so I felt confident that I could handle it. Perhaps not confident enough to completely quell the fingers of anxiety playing up and down my spine.

At that moment the surgery barn door opened. The head of department and a group of foreign visitors entered. They had been touring the premises all morning and had chosen this, my first moment in the limelight, to visit surgery.

My senior colleague, instructor and mentor, a man of many years experience in equine anesthesia, stepped to my side. "I'll do this one. You take the next." He wanted to shield me from performance anxiety before this august audience. Taking the syringe of barbiturate anesthetic I was holding, he swapped it for the large rubber tube he had in his hands ready to pass into the horse's windpipe as soon as it lost consciousness. That in turn would be connected to an anesthetic machine to deliver a carefully monitored dose of anesthetic gases.

Horses are strange creatures. Huge as they are, they allow themselves to be dominated and controlled by beings a fraction of their size. Sometimes we forget the disparity in weight and strength. They can sleep standing by locking the tendons in their legs. And they are entirely unpredictable.

My colleague injected the anesthetic. The audience stood quietly to one side.

We expected our patient to sink quietly to the rubber mat after the barbiturate injection. The role of the man at its head was mainly to hold tight to the head collar rope to soften the fall of its head onto the thick rubber mat.

This horse was not usual. Keeping its head up, its forelegs stiffened and its hind legs folded under its body. The technician was jerked forward, lost his balance but held onto the head-rope. The horse's rump hit the floor; and its body flipped over backwards. The technician was thrown across the room into the wall. Without restraint the horse's head came down with a sickening thump, missed the padded rubber floor and hit the concrete surrounding the casting area. As it rolled onto its side it folded its legs up to its belly and shuddered.

We acted as a team to grasp the head, open the mouth, insert the tube and connect it to the anesthetic machine. The technician, a little dazed, reached us as we started to remove the horse's protective clothing.

The patient appeared to be breathing easily and there seemed to be no untoward effects of its dramatic fall. We dragged it into position on the mat and, once stable, handed the patient over to the surgeon.

The surgery proceeded uneventfully.

With the surgery complete it was our job as anesthetists to monitor the animal's vital signs as it returned to consciousness and prevent the horse damaging himself during recovery. This he could do by trying to stand too early whilst still under the influence of the anesthetic drugs. We would support him until we felt he could stand on his own. Then, once back on his feet, assist him to balance until he was capable of walking unaided.

Usually this did not take too long. By the end of surgery the normal patient has usually metabolized the injectable drugs to the point where they will no longer keep him asleep and he has merely to breathe out the inhaled gases.

Our patient slept on. An hour after surgery he showed no signs of regaining consciousness. He slept through the afternoon. We had by now established an intravenous drip, and rolled him from side to side periodically to improve air and blood flow in the lungs. Still he did not stir.

We set up a clinical rotation to monitor him through the night.

He did not wake up.

Two days later the unconscious horse was painlessly destroyed and autopsied.

The horse had a fractured neck at the base of the skull

where it joined the spine.

Now the problems began. Unfortunately the horse had not been insured for surgery so the owner wished to redeem his financial loss through legal means. However, the owner had signed a pre-surgical statement acknowledging the possibility of a host of things that could go wrong, including a fatality. At that time a claim for malpractice required obvious evidence of negligence. My colleague, firmly established in the profession, was able to demonstrate that several other schools of veterinary medicine used a technique identical to the one he had used on this horse. He was also able to produce nearly a thousand records of horses he had successfully anesthetized without a problem using the same technique used on this most unfortunate animal.

This would not have been the case had I administered the fateful anesthetic dose. I had no experience whatsoever. My future would have been hanging by a thread. If there were a future.

There were many lessons to be learned. Every procedure entails a real risk of misadventure. Horses are big and heavy and they can hurt people and themselves even in the hands of the most experienced handlers. It is sensible, if ones financial investment in an animal is substantial, to take the precaution to cover possible losses through insurance.

And it behooves new graduates to choose a dependable mentor. One who recognizes that there are times when the urge to get on with a procedure must take second place to common sense.

Thank you, my friend.

Commentary

Christiaan Barnard performed the world's first heart-lung transplant on Louis Washkansky on December 3rd 1967 at Groote Schuur Hospital in South Africa. Donald Ross, also South African born, performed the first British heart-lung transplant in a human patient on May 3rd 1968 at the National Heart Hospital, London.

That year I received the post graduate Diploma in Anaesthesia of the Royal College of Veterinary Surgeons.

The following years in academia and at a research institute were fairly serious. I do not remember many humorous tales from this period, although I learned a great deal about human behavior. I cannot possibly predict whether it will infuse itself into the following chapters.

Between academia and the world of practice, I spent a period of reorientation at the Animal Medical Center in New York City, as a resident in surgery.

The days at the AMC sometimes stretched into the late evening hours. And in the spirit of the Bare Skin Ladies, I would occasionally cross paths with Sharylyn walking her beat at the intersection close to my apartment. Although she didn't have a dog with her, she usually greeted me with—how shall I put it?—encouragement. This wasn't the type of relationship I was looking for, but after a few encounters, if she had some downtime, we exchanged the time of night, in a purely neighborly fashion you understand. Then I ventured to ask her why she prowled the area at weekends.

"Oh," she said. "I do this part time. During the week I'm a secretary."

It gave a whole new meaning to moonlighting.

16

Sammi

*If I can stop one heart from breaking,
I shall not live in vain.* ~ *Emily Dickinson*

I was startled awake by my bedside telephone. Reflexes guided my hand to the telephone, my hand to my ear. I glanced at the bleary red figures on the bedside clock. It read 1:00 a.m.

"Sorry to wake you. This is Dr. Myers. I have admitted a serious bite wound."

I recognized the voice as the intern o duty at the Animal Medical Center in New York City.

Throwing back the covers I tried to gather my sleepy wits the better to hear about the case, and answer this unspoken plea for help.

Damn, who allows his dog to be bitten at this hour of the night?

"It's a poodle, sixteen years old. Big dog--little dog syndrome."

These encounters usually cause horrible wounds to the smaller of the two. A big dog grasps a little one by the neck, the back, or any convenient place, and shakes him like a terrier shakes a rat. The skin may tear. More often than not the long canine teeth leave small puncture holes in the skin, which mask severe damage to the muscles and body wall below, ripped and lacerated as the victim's body is shaken to and fro in the assailant's jaws. Not a case I looked forward to, and I had worn a stethoscope as a badge of office for many more years than the intern.

"How's he doing?" I asked.

"She," he answered. "Her chest's badly lacerated. Part of a lung is sticking out of one of the wounds. Big time trouble breathing. She's pretty shocky. Not too responsive. Oh, and she's on treatment for congestive heart failure."

Before I can ask if he thought the dog had any chance of survival, he added, "The owner wants everything possible done. Putting her to sleep is out of the question."

"Right. Okay, I'll be right over."

Still holding the telephone to my ear, I scrambled into clothes while the intern told me he had already started an intravenous fluid drip, placed a mask on the dog's nose so she could breathe oxygen and started medical therapy for shock. I ran down the four flights of stairs from my apartment muttering under my breath, hoping that my car was still parked outside.

As an intern, Dr. Myers was enjoying and suffering through the first year of his professional life. This is not an easy period. Fresh from school, having survived an arduous selection process for one of the few internship positions available in the country, he could expect to rack up a huge sleep deficit during the next year. For eighty hours a week he would learn to convert the wealth of facts crammed into his skull into a practical clinical approach. Licensed professional he may be, but no one expected him to be able to handle severe trauma or thoracic surgery fresh out of school. Particularly alone in the middle of the night.

I knew it would be a battle to save this patient, if she hadn't died by the time I reached the hospital. There were already three strikes against her; her age, heart condition, and the severity of her wounds. Even if we could pull her through the immediate surgery, infection was always a danger with dog bites.

There was never a shortage of trauma cases at the AMC, one of the busiest small animal hospitals in the U.S. The 'hit-by-car' case used to be the most common, until strictly enforced leash laws brought about a dramatic decline in their number. The 'high-rise' syndrome was another urban problem; the victim, usually a cat, falls from an open window. There were always fight and bite wounds.

Parked below the AMC building, I rang the doorbell, and waited impatiently for the night-duty receptionist to scan me on the television camera and release the door lock. The race up the ramp to the first floor, through reception, past the empty examination area and down the long hallway to surgery stretched far longer than usual.

Light reflected from the surface of the stainless steel table in the surgical prep-room where my patient, a small apricot colored poodle, lay on a blanket. Her pale coat was matted and soiled with a mix of blood and dirt, in addition to her assailant's saliva. The intern had the dog's nose buried in the cone of an oxygen mask. A tube snaked up from her front leg to a bottle of fluid suspended above the table. The chest wounds were hidden under an untidy bandage, hastily placed to seal off the openings. There were no other visible wounds. Her breathing was definitely labored. My first task was to keep her alive. To examine the wounds, I had to remove the bandage holding the dressing over the hole in her chest wall, the only thing that was enabling her to breathe at all.

She looked so tiny and vulnerable. The slightest struggle I feared would end this poor little mite's life. The annoying case of twenty minutes before was now my patient. I was damned if I would let her die without a struggle.

I injected an anesthetic into the intravenous line, passed a tube through her mouth into her trachea and connected it to an anesthetic machine powered by a ventilator. The machine could now do the work of breathing for her while keeping her unconscious.

There were two lacerations and several puncture wounds on the left side of her chest. Behind the foreleg, a piece of lung protruded through one of the tears, its own blood supply cut off, the delicate sponge like tissue collapsed and discolored. It sealed the leak but also trapped air in the cavity of the chest compressing the lungs. To give this little dog any chance, the chest wall had to be repaired, any tears in the lung sealed, and the chest cavity evacuated of blood and air. As the surgical technician on duty clipped the hair away from the wounds and scrubbed the site for surgery I went to meet the owner.

On a bench in the waiting room, empty and silent at this hour, he sat alone, withering in sorrow beneath a heavy coat, his face hidden in the shadows of a hat. Like his pet, he was in his twilight years. I knew without asking that the patient being readied in surgery was his only companion. This is the hardest combination when one has to explain the medical and surgical dilemma facing the pet. Any threat to the pet was a threat to her owner. I was about to step on their empathetic bond, and possibly sunder it forever, a move which also exposed his own age and vulnerability.

"How is my Sammi?" he asked. "Will she be all right?"

"You call her Sammy?"

"Her name's spelled with an 'i'."

He was anxious to tell me how she was as a young dog, full of life and vitality. As he talked his face brightened with memories he could hold on to—to keep Sammi alive in his mind. The old dog became a pup again, bounding about, fetching a ball, doing tricks, begging, rolling over and playing dead. He told me how she pretended to be an alarm clock in the morning, jumping up on the bed and licking his face.

"Can't do that anymore. Bed's too high for her now."

He did not want to hear bad news. As he relived Sammi's puppyhood, I could understand why he would not be able to accept it. I explained about the chest injury, about her heart condition and her age, and the influence they could have on the outcome. Before any heroic attempts were made I had to find out what his true wishes were. Gently I explained the choices. We did have the option to bring Sammi's life to a quiet close. The old man understood, but he urged me to try and save her. He could not face a parting so sudden, so unexpected. The shock of her injury was agonizing. The thought of losing his closest companion of sixteen years, unbearable.

"Do the surgery, Doctor, I'll wait here."

As I turned to go, a hand caught my sleeve. I looked down at wet eyes begging for understanding.

"Doc, Sammi always comes, Doc. She maybe didn't hear me. She went right up to the other dog." He paused. "She didn't come. Sammi didn't come." The old man sighed as he, remembered. "She was only shook once. The other dog dropped her when he was told."

"The other dog listened to you?" I asked.

"No, his owner."

"His owner?"

"Yes, he had him on a leash. A Doberman. It wasn't his fault. I didn't have Sammi on a leash."

He had felt it safe to leave Sammi unleashed. No longer a spritely young thing, she would plod quietly along beside him. The rushing-around days were long gone when she would explore all the new sights and smells that a walk with her master and friend had to offer. To his grief, he had added a burden of guilt.

The operating lamps glared down on the small body. The hair from the base of the neck to the middle of the abdomen had been clipped away. The skin scrubbed with an iodine solution turning it a golden brown color, merging at the edges into the apricot coat. The technician was opening the surgical pack on the instrument table. The ventilator rhythmically inflated and deflated the chest. With each breath air hissed from around the protruding lung. The beep-beep of the cardiac monitor and the quiet hiss of the vacuum lines added to the familiar operating room sounds.

I checked the ventilator settings, examined the dog's color and eye reflexes, adjusted the drip and moved into the adjacent scrub room. As I lathered my hands and forearms, I reflected that Sammi had held her own so far. Now it would be up to me to give her all the help I could. Back into the operating room, I draped the patient and started surgery.

The surgery went swiftly as I cut away the discolored muscle and fat leaving healthy tissue, and cleaned away the hair. I attached the ribs back to the spine with thin stainless steel wires, and pulled them together to close the gaping hole in her side. The chest was sucked clear of fluid. I placed a long plastic drainage tube in the chest leading to the outside and blew nitrous oxide, an anesthetic gas, into the cavity to replace the air before I stitched the wound closed. When the skin edges were together, I sucked out most of the gas; the rest would be rapidly absorbed and breathed out with the other anesthetic gases. Then began the process of weaning the patient from the ventilator. As soon as I was sure Sammi was able to breathe on her own, I walked back to the waiting room to talk to the owner. I was suddenly aware that fatigue had caught up to me. The light of early dawn smudged the windows grey.

The owner had aged during the night, or perhaps it was the harsh early light that cast thin shadows outlining his wrinkled face. I told him how Sammi had overcome the first hurdle. Although he would be lonely for days, he knew his pet now had a chance to hold on to life.

Sammi survived. She was helped by daily visits from her owner. Sometimes twice a day. Even in her pain, every visit had an effect. Sammi lifted her ears, used her tail to signal her love, and, I swear, she tried to smile. This was repeated so many times while she was in the hospital. After days of intensive care, when the drainage from the chest had stopped and the chest tube had been removed, when the pain had subsided enough to let the dog pay attention to more than the agony of breathing, and all infection was controlled, Sammi at last went home.

As with many cases that needed care for so long, the

nursing crews, the technicians and all the staff who dealt with her, while happy for her recovery, still suffered a sense of loss when she left to go home.

The emotional attachment they felt is not hard to explain. In human practice it's called the Florence Nightingale Effect, after 'The Lady with the Lamp,' where patients may bond with their caregivers and vice versa. It has been suggested that in humans it is due to the patient mistaking a caring bedside manner for a romantic interest. In this case, our patient would not have been mistaken. The staff truly loved her.

17

Spacey Medicine

Never attribute to malice that which can be adequately explained by stupidity. ~ Hanlon's razor.

While reading the notices on the message board, my tech handed me a patient chart.

Someone had pinned up a quotation from the paper—Graffiti "Don't be scared to ask dumb questions, it's better than making dumb mistakes."

I was still smiling about it as I entered the examination room. My client, a young lady, dressed in student uniform of jeans, sloppy sweatshirt, and climbing boots (they were all the rage), her brow furrowed above glistening eyes, held a tiny kitten.

I introduced myself and she mumbled her name in reply. Despite my sometimes slow awareness of emotional states, I detected that she was more concerned with her pet than the niceties of social discourse.

"How's she been doing?"

"I don't know, doctor. She's not been acting right. Not like any kitten I've had before."

I read the previous entry in the clinical record. The patient was barely six weeks old, a foundling from a shelter, presented three days before for an upper respiratory infection.

"Sneezing still?" I asked.

"It's not that. The kitten's ..." She shrugged, "peculiar."

Such an explicit description. I sighed. However, this was my last patient for the evening, so I could afford to be tolerant.

She placed the kitten on the table and I watched the little shrimp.

Its legs were stiff as it walked on the cold stainless steel of the examination table, a pound of gray fluff, bristling all over as if tumble-dried with fabric softener. Its tail stood straight up like a bottlebrush. The eyes stared with wide blue wonder. They were rimmed by a pink film that matted the lids. Small blobs of goo adhered to the inner margins. Damp patches stained the sides of the nose.

"Let's take a look." I started the physical examination.

Even when standing still the kitten was in constant motion, its body quivering with a fine tremor. The stare of blue-eyed wonder was unfocused. The kitten took no notice of my hand moving in its visual field. This kitten was spaced out!

"How long has she been acting this way?"

"About two days. It's been getting worse."

The rest of the examination yielded no further useful information. I had a kitty on a high. Maybe it found a stash. Far out! Now it was up to me to discover the truth—by questions astute and adroit—so as not to send the owner scurrying to her attorney complaining that I had accused her of using recreational drugs, or worse yet, feeding them to her kitty.

"Has she been taking her medication?" I asked innocently.

"Yes." The owner paused. "She doesn't like it much. I can put the drops in her eyes, but the capsules are a real struggle to get down her."

Alarm bells sounded in my mind. Drops? Capsules? I checked again the medication prescribed by my colleague at the earlier visit. Chloramphenicol *eye ointment* four times daily and pediatric antibiotic drops (amoxicillin 0.25 ml) *by mouth* twice daily. No capsules. Oops!

"May I take a look at what you've been giving her?" My voice was calm, but my mind was whirling.

She handed over two packets. One contained an antibiotic, amoxicillin drops, and the other contained chloramphenicol *capsules*, 250mg, one by mouth four times daily. No eye ointment!

I glanced again at the kitty's red-rimmed eyes. It had been getting the strawberry flavored oral medication in its eyes—through no fault of the owner—and the capsules by mouth. Somewhere the dispensing system had broken down.

First, I must attend to the kitten.

Mumbling sweet nothings to the ball of fluff, I killed time by using damp cotton to wash the medication off the kitten's eyelids. I gave the problem of how to explain the kitten's condition to my subconscious while I performed mathematic gymnastics in my head. The dose for chloramphenicol is 4.5 to 11 mg/kg three times daily—ergo, this kitten had been poisoned with 40 to 100 times that dose.

I performed the 'winning smile' ceremony that usually accompanies the fee. "You are absolutely right," I said with conviction.

The owner stared back with a half-smile of incomprehension.

"Your kitten *is* acting strange. Sort of spacey. Can you see that?" I turned the shrimp toward her and waved at the bristling fur. "I think that it's reacting to the medication in an unusual way."

We agreed to stop all treatment for a day or so. The owner was to observe and call with daily progress reports. I intended to find out who had done what before muddying the waters with excuses or accusations. Recriminations could be pursued when we had found out if the kitten would recover or suffer any permanent damage.

Epilogue

The kitten came down to earth in a day or so. It even recovered from the upper respiratory infection. The owner was relieved and as bright eyed and bushy tailed as her kitten. The matter had been taken up with the pharmacy by someone several pay-grades above me, effectively taking it out of my hands, so I decided to let the sleeping dog lie—or its kitten equivalent.

Our dispensing procedures suddenly bristled with checks and balances, and a new notice had been pinned on the bulletin board.

Give the right dose
Of the right drug
To the right patient
By the right route
At the right time.

Underneath someone had written 'Right on.'

18

Footling Around

Speak in French when you can't think of the English for a thing. ~ The Red Queen, in Through the Looking Glass, Lewis Carroll

"It's time you settled down."

I was being addressed by my distant aunt. The one I call Aunt Josephine. We're related by marriage, whose I am not sure. It's all hidden in that immigrant genealogy thing, and name changes at Ellis Island. We had not known each other long. When we met, she 'evaluated' me to establish my suitability to be recognized as a member of her extended family. It could have been a job appraisal, she was so thorough yet I felt more like a squirrel being invited to lunch by a hawk. The time of her questioning fell during a period of readjustment in my life, at the beginning of my re-entry into practice. A change in marital status, or being recycled after a two year re-acquaintance with bachelorhood, was also in the cards.

In appearance, to be generous, Aunt Josephine presented herself as the classic example of a motherly aunt, her skeleton amply covered, rounded so to say, a shape that skillfully disguised her attitude towards life, and anyone who dared to trample on her aura. Despite her reassuring appearance, one that suggested softness comfort and reliance—an aunt any young child between ten and forty years could rely on—doubts might arise at the sight of her hair. She invariably wore it woven into a tightly coiled bun, held fiercely above her neck between her ears, as if daring it to move. I assumed at first that its color was natural, a cold steel grey, but it showed in spots that it had the potential to soften into silver if she would ever to allow it. Unlike her hair, her eyebrows dared to be different; they proclaimed that she had once been a redhead.

"Have you stopped footling around yet?" she continued with the vehemence of stamping a mental foot. Answering that was like trying to answer 'have you stopped beating your wife?' But let us first understand 'footling.'

To footle: Intransitive Verb. *To fool around or waste time, trifle. To talk nonsense.*

A variant of footer, probably from French foutre, to copulate with, from old French.

What?

That could be interpreted as me ******* around. What an amazing verb, *to footle*, one I had previously accepted as an *innocent* way to waste time. However, being generous and magnanimous in nature, I granted Auntie a general understanding of the word although I doubted if her comprehensive knowledge included the suggested Old French origin.

"How on earth did you ever earn a position in a university in the first place," she said. Although phrased as a question it was made as a statement. "You seem to me to be entirely too scattered in thought."

She sounded like Lady Bracknell in The Importance of Being Ernest, and as did characters such as Lady Bracknell, my aunt's attitude could bring out the worst in me. Perhaps not the worst, but worse than my usual sanguine self. I had been on the faculty of two universities, had no idea which one she had in mind and did not care to find out. It could double the confusion of her interrogation.

"I was offered the position when I was at a NATO meeting in Brussels," I snapped. This was stretching the truth a tad because if I remember correctly, I was told about the university position in a bar at a meeting in Cambridge, by an American Professor swilling his third or fourth martini.

"Phooey! What would someone like you be doing at a NATO conference?"

"Sorry, can't talk about it. Official Secrets Act."

For a moment she was speechless, so before she could retort I added "All I can tell you is that I was doing research on sheep on a remote island, where the army had some sort of facility or other a missile tracking station I believe." That fact was common knowledge, but she was not to know that. "But I am not allowed to discuss that."

She stared at me, her expression as close to incredulous as I imagined she could express. "Are you telling me you signed The British Official Secrets Act?"

I maintained a passive visage, trying to be inscrutable. To sign the Official Secrets Act merely means that one has signed a government document committing one to secrecy on pain of prosecution as a traitor, death perhaps, or something equally dastardly. I had been expected to do this, a formality I was told, when I spent a month on said remote island actually studying sheep. However, in true British Government fashion, the aforementioned document relating to 'never revealing classified sheep' or army information relating thereto, hadn't arrived before I left on the trip. It was awaiting me on my return, but by then the whole episode was over so I didn't bother. No one followed up. This I did not intend to tell Aunt Josephine, but as I did not want to lie outright, I remained silent with my eyes scrunched in inscrutability.

The NATO conference, and the visit to the remote island as part of a research team, had nothing whatsoever to do with each other. In fact they occurred some years apart. Again, I did not enlighten Auntie.

I was reminded of this exchange with my aunt on reading a book, years later, by Christopher Andrew and Vasili Mitrokhin, *The Sword and The Shield, the Mitrokhin Archive*, about the secret history of the KGB. I had this rather late epiphany—I understood now why the NATO conference in Brussels had been so important. At the time I had been in charge of a unit where sheep were raised isolated from one another in a sterile environment so that they were quite free of pathogenic organisms that could interfere with research on particular diseases—now I realized the operative word was *isolation*. That's why NATO was involved. They were more concerned about the techniques I used to safely raise the sheep. That included those experimentally infected with nasty germs so that they didn't infect others in the isolation unit. I had naively and innocently contributed basic research knowledge that could have helped with biological warfare.

Good Heavens! I had possibly been in the presence of spooks. My notes copied, pored over and smuggled as microdots to foreign parties. *How to isolate sheep. Classified. Eyes only.* It was powerful and heady stuff. I might even have been under surveillance. When did it end? Had it ended? I peered carefully around the curtain and surveyed the road. Oh shut up!

NATO and the Official Secrets Act had effectively stifled the questions about what I intended to do with my life. I had not so far told her that I was awaiting the outcome of a job application while I finished up a two year residency to re-orient myself to clinical practice. Or that I was limiting my search area because of a romantic interest—a mutual interest actually—after all it is difficult for a person to marry *alone*, it always involves at least two. With Auntie's question about my future parried, she retired to regroup, or re-gird her voluminous loins, as it were.

But, back to the hiatus of academia. It had made me wonder, that if there were official secrets, what qualified as an unofficial secret? My growing relationship to 'my lady-friend' perhaps? You understand if I withhold her name until the secrecy matter is decided. How does one make a secret official? Is there a form to fill out? Please Sir or Auntie, I wish to make the following secret, that I do not wish you to know about, into an Official Secret, so that I may not tell you. Like everyone else, including me, Auntie would have to wait and see.

The short period of sheep research, on said remote, 'not to be talked about' island revealed a twisted side to military logic. To reach the island we relied on the army to transport us there by ship, in our case a converted minesweeper. Among the army personnel on board was a newly minted physician about to spend two years in rural isolation, with the isolated men and sheep, on the isolated island. This period of his army service was the cost of being offered the opportunity to be trained for a higher degree to become a specialist at the army's expense. In his case, in gynecology.

The only women he might hope to encounter would be Russian trawler skippers. However, the island was recognized as an international aid station, despite its isolation and secrecy. Thus it had a fully equipped medical outfit—a metal hut with the essentials—and our new Doctor. Shortly after our arrival he showed us round, as much to explore the facility as show it off. He opened a storage room. The shelves, floor to ceiling, held instruments, creams, and other articles of obstetric equipment.

I can imagine the bureaucrat making the assignment. "Found where we send all that obstetric stuff. Better send the new man there."

I doubt if I will ever understand logic. To me it's a secret. But then again, as the doctor's posting was an army decision, the officer deciding his fate may have swilled too many martinis and have simply been 'footling around.'

19

Cat Speak

Speak the speech, I pray you, as I pronounc'd it to you, trippingly on the tongue. ~ Hamlet, William Shakespeare

"Of course cats can talk!" Anne said. She was quite adamant. Young teenage girls are, aren't they? They wouldn't be normal otherwise.

"Really?" I may have put a little too much sarcastic spin on that question. But baiting people can be fun sometimes.

She had gone on to explain. "Yes, I mean they always tell what they want."

I had then made the mistake of relating the conversation to her mother, up to that point quite a dear friend. Oh hush my foolish tongue. There is sometimes a place for editorial comment—judging by the TV news and Aunt Josephine—sometimes not. I chose unwisely. "Some never ever grow out of believing that cats can talk," I said.

The apple whistled past my ear, confirming the adage that silence is preferable to an unwise choice. However I was trying to make a point. She knew I was referring to her daughter, and perhaps herself. I vowed to be more cautious in future. Mothers are so emotionally volatile, not taking time to think, acting on reflex, and throwing apples and things. You won't tell her I said that, will you!

"Beau talks," Anne had continued—Anne being, as I said earlier, the aforementioned volatile mother's teenage daughter—referring to a large black and white domestic short haired cat. "He throws himself on his back on the floor in front of you if he wants something, like cantaloupe."

"Cantaloupe?" I would have to try this.

"And Samantha whistles."

"Of course."

Problem is, she was almost right—perhaps a little more than almost, because not long after that, I looked out of the window and saw Samantha, the other talking cat, stalking in the grass. It took a while for me to figure out her quarry. She obviously didn't know what she was after. It was a woodchuck, at least twice her size. Suddenly it sat up and looked at the small crouching putty cat.

Sam took a second or two to size up the situation. It was not good. She peered around, spotted Beau on a tree, lifted her head in the air and sauntered towards him as if any idea she harbored about seizing dinner, a four course dinner in this case, had never existed. And she whistled, as if it were the most natural thing in the world, I'll swear she whistled. A feline Gene Kelly skipping through the puddles. There I admit it; Anne was almost right.

I wondered how Beau had climbed the tree. He was a feline klutz. His attempts at such youthful antics usually left him spread-eagled on the trunk like Garfield on a car window. Maybe his athletic ability had been encouraged by seeing Sam's woodchuck. We had to carry him down later.

Then I remembered that a long time ago, I had learned that cats let you know their desires. It must have been a repressed memory, like the mind quarantining junk mail, or deleting messages it didn't want others to read. I thought back to my student days. The time when I was painfully learning how to figure out farmers, and what to wear when visiting young pigs, and how to clip wool, and all manner of arcane practices that were a far cry from my intended professional life with horses.

I was at Alan Saunders's house, well a small farm really, where he bred South Devon cattle. By bovine standards they are among the bigger critters. As a breed they are so called dual purpose animals, used both for milk and doubling as a Sunday roast or a sandwich filling. At least as big as a horse, in many cases bigger. Well there I was, wandering up to the house, when I saw the herd of breakfast and lunch material crowded at the gate into a field, or out of it depending on which way you were going. They wanted out and the gate was open. But they would not come through.

As I drew closer I saw Alan's Siamese cat sitting on the gate post. The cat appeared totally unconcerned about the cows. However it was obvious the cows were concerned about the cat, and would not pass.

I wheedled the story from him later. One day, he told me, the cat was sitting in the middle of the gate as the cows approached. Being quite bovine and dumb, those in the lead were suspicious of the cat, lowered their heads and sniffed at it. The cat responded with a feline defensive move, drawing blood with a swift one-two, left and right hooks to the nose. Another cow took the first victim's place to challenge the cat, and another. Between opponents, the cat licked his paws and washed his face. Soon there were no more cows prepared to take the Siamese challenge. Cowed by their feline aggressor, the animals reached an understanding. When the cat was present, the cows would not pass.

Later that evening I sat in the sitting room reading up on mysterious farm practices. The cat lay in front of the fire. I stood up to change my reading material, a different farming magazine, swapping cattle for pigs, or vice versa, and in passing I stroked the cat.

"Shouldn't do that," said Alan. " He doesn't like it."

"Oh," I bit back the expletive that usually follows as the cat stalked over to me and demonstrated his bovine attack move with a swift one two to my shins. Then he stalked back to the fireplace, grinned at me, and curled up on the rug.

I went down to the cow barn and explained to the

cows that I now understood. I really did.

"Do you like cats?" Anne said.
"Of course," I answered a little too quickly.
I showed my love by throwing pieces of cantaloupe to Beau later that evening. It was fun until Anne's mother slipped on the mess on the floor and naturally the darn cat let me down by having diarrhea all over the place the next day.

Now, years later, I talk to my cat regularly, a lot more than many professed cat lovers, even my therapist says so. We have developed quite a vocabulary between us, but he is better at understanding my cat than I am at understanding his—let's admit it—rather feeble attempts at human speech. But I can't scold him, because he is so grateful that he shares his supper with me, at least the less digestible portions of it that he gets from some personal kitty market outside. He likes to eat in bed.

But sometimes when he tells me, usually around three am, that he has an invitation to another block party and could he please go out, I wish I had never met Anne. But then I would never have married her mother.

20

One for You, One for Me

Friends share all things. ~ *Pythagoras.*

During the hiatus I alluded to before, a time when I was in a period of readjustment, at the beginning of my re-entry into practice after leaving the AMC, I worked in a practice some miles from home. If I call it home, that is purely for convenience, you understand. It was the home I would soon share with my future spouse type person on being recycled, and her daughter Anne with the talking cats. This living arrangement required that I maintain an apartment somewhere near the practice to crash during on-call nights and weekends. The one I rented matched my lifestyle, primitive but functional.

I had barely entered the door to my apartment after a tedious day at the practice—long enough to start stripping the wrapping from a nameless and unidentifiable cardboard box that claimed to be an incredibly satisfying dinner—when the phone jangled my nerves back to the present.

"I think my puppy drank some antifreeze."

With a great effort I dismissed my right brain fantasies of relaxation, music and good food, or at least an expensive TV dinner. An easy task as there was a serious deficit of electronic entertainment equipment. The apartment lacked a TV, a stereo or even a transistor radio.

"When and how much?" I asked, knowing that three tablespoons of this poison can kill a medium sized dog, and the owner was describing a puppy.

"I'm not sure. I think he drank some before I got home, but I am not sure."

"What is he doing?"

"Doing?"

"How is he acting?"

"Like he always does."

I thrust the feelings of hunger and hypoglycemia into the background. The owner had already told me a lot. If his pup was still acting normally, there were two options—either he really hadn't drunk any, or the owner had caught the problem early, possibly within thirty minutes. There was no time to waste.

"Bring him in," I said.

"Why?"

"Antifreeze is extremely poisonous. It damages the kidneys very quickly,"

Struggling not to drop the telephone squeezed between my ear and shoulder I fought the insistent cramp in my neck.

"Can it wait till morning?" he said.

I gave up the unequal battle between the slipping phone and cramp. Changing the phone to one hand, the box to the other I tried to convince him to bring the pup in, while stuffing the right object in the microwave, and nuking my evening meal.

"If he has drunk antifreeze he needs treatment right away," I said.

"What can you do?"

I fumbled with my cardboard box and told him his pup needed an intravenous injection of a drug to block the antifreeze from changing into a more dangerous compound that caused kidney damage.

"Okay."

"Okay? Okay, what?"

"I will bring him in."

We set a mutually agreeable time, one that meant be here ASAP.

I chewed on a little of the lukewarm semi-nuked TV delight. It tasted like a cardboard box. With a deep sigh, I dragged on my coat and headed out the door.

The success of treating this type of poisoning is dependent on how much the pet has drunk, and how much time has gone by since it drank it. The longer the time between drinking and treatment, the more antifreeze will have been changed into toxic compounds. These are first products which cause an acid overload in the body, then these are transformed into calcium oxalate.

The treatment is to give the patient straight ethyl alcohol to stop the ethylene glycol in the antifreeze from being metabolized. Once in the kidneys, calcium oxalate can damage these vital organs irreversibly. Sodium bicarbonate is used to counteract the acid overload.

I reached the practice. I could find no ethyl alcohol.

Before my left brain accepted the status quo—that's Latin for you are in deep doo-doo baby—the client arrived with an adorable Labrador puppy.

It was alert, chewing, exploring, peeing. There was no vomiting, depression or lack of balance, which meant he hadn't drunk antifreeze, or it was less than 30 minutes since he drank it. And I couldn't fault his owner, he really was concerned. The pup had possibly found a puddle of coolant that had leaked from his neighbor's car, because he was outside, playing with the kids when Dad arrived home.

"When did you get home?" I asked.

"Right before I called you."

That put it about half an hour before, give or take a bit.

I admitted the little scrap into the hospital, put him in a cage, reassured the owner about my incredible skill and knowledge—I did not tell him we had no alcohol –and sent him on his way. There was no neighboring practice on call. The nearest referral center was over an hour away. The pup was stuck with me. Now I was developing the jitters.

What could I do about alcohol? Many a good man has asked that. The nearest I could reckon was vodka. I didn't have any vodka. I had no idea where a liquor store might be. And I didn't think to check the phonebook. I climbed into the car and burned rubber to the nearest watering hole, a pick up spot for the lonely, the single and the rejected—and alcohol seeking veterinarians.

I like to think that I sidled up to the bar like the hero does in movies when he wants to impress. I didn't. My approach was in more of a begging frame of mind.

"I need a bottle of vodka," I said, holding my imaginary begging bowl. "Urgently."

"We can't sell liquor," he replied. "We can only serve it here, in the bar." That meant buying a bottle shot by shot.

Undeterred, I felt I should look meaningfully around the bar, hitch up my metaphorical gun-belt and lean toward him. I settled on the last bit.

"This is the problem," I stammered in my best Bogie voice. I am not sure Bogie ever felt anxious, but if he did, his voice, like mine, might have risen an octave or two.

Fortunately the barman understood and accommodated my request. To cover his ... protect his actions, I signed a quickly written, partially legal and semi-notarized document that we scribbled on a placemat stating that I desperately needed a bottle of vodka for medical purposes. He was satisfied that his nether end was suitably covered. I translated: He didn't believe me, but he didn't care either way. I scrambled out of the bar.

Back at the clinic I started treatment. By first figuring out the equivalent dose of vodka. If vodka is 80 proof, that is 40% alcohol—oh this was too easy—and I needed 20%. So....

He was so small, this tiny vulnerable puppy. This provided problem number one. Try as I might, single handed, and with a wriggling happy pup, placing an intravenous catheter into a vein was beyond me. But I could pass a stomach tube single handed. I daren't waste any more time, so I gave him a dose of vodka, through a stomach tube to see what might happen. A few minutes passed then he grinned—you do know puppies can grin, right? He sighed, passed out and rolled on his back.

After twenty minutes or so he raised his head, shook off the hangover—that must have hurt—rolled onto his tummy and wagged his tail. I decided to divide the hourly dose rate and go with that by mouth, alternating bicarbonate and vodka.

I repeated the treatment. He passed out. I waited. He woke up. He wagged his tail. I gave him another dose. He passed out.

This is where I really felt it should be one for him, one for me.

We binged the night away.

One for you – unfortunately none for me.

In the morning the boss found me asleep with the puppy. My mouth tasted like the bottom of a cardboard box.

"Why didn't you put a catheter in a vein when he was unconscious?" he asked.

"The stomach tube method appeared to work okay," I said, kicking myself.

The early office calls staggered in. The puppy wanted attention. He wagged his tail. He showed no signs of having drunk anything other than what I had given him. The treatment was meant to continue through the day, but we hadn't been open long when the owner arrived.

"Sorry I bothered you Doc. That stuff the puppy drank–it wasn't antifreeze. I don't know. Something one of the kids spilled from art class."

The frustration at having stayed up all night could match my relief that the pup really hadn't been poisoned.

I think now that I *should* have shared my patient's treatment. It *should* have been one for you, one for me.

The puppy, bright as a button—perhaps I should say as button-like as one can be with a severe hangover—left for home. I looked for the vodka. Gone! The boss had taken it.

After morning calls I swayed home, not quite as bright

as a button. An empty cardboard box lay in wait on my kitchen counter.

***

Any levity in this situation was aimed at my condition because antifreeze poisoning is nothing to make light of.

All animals can be poisoned by drinking radiator antifreeze which is 95% ethylene glycol. Unfortunately, it is most common in dogs and cats. Every year more than ten thousand of our pets fall victim to this poison. One small sip can be fatal.

Cats are much more sensitive to the poison than dogs. The minimum lethal dose of undiluted ethylene glycol is 1.4 ml/kg body wt in cats, 4.4 ml/kg in dogs, which translates to a lethal dose of radiator antifreeze of about 1 ½ tablespoons of antifreeze for a ten pound puppy; 1 ½ teaspoons for a ten pound cat

The puppy in this story was not showing any clinical signs of intoxication. Had he drunk antifreeze, it would have been within half an hour of him being brought in. It can be asked why I did not make the puppy vomit first. Sometimes you do what you can. My shortcoming was that I could not treat him intravenously. Vomiting could have screwed up trying to treat him by mouth.

21

Temperature Rising

Haste trips up its own heels. ~ John Wanamaker

The call came at ten-thirty p.m. as I arrived home from the practice—from a colleague—he wanted his thermometer back. Oops! I checked our dog's behind where she lay on a towel sleeping off an anesthetic. The thermometer still read 104, high, even for one of my patients.

I still worked in the vodka-free practice, and although by now Helen and I had re-tied our previously severed love knots, working arrangements had changed little. It was not unusual for me to be away for several days at a time. Earlier that evening I had arrived back after an absence of a few days to be told by one of the kids that our dog Dulcinea was sick. She lay about, wouldn't eat. I checked her over. Of course I didn't have a thermometer at home--it was at the practice. When I lifted her muzzle it obviously caused pain. I tried to open her mouth, and she resisted strongly. Ha! Super sleuth had a good idea where the problem lay.

The way to find out would be to examine her mouth more thoroughly. Dulcie had no intention of cooperating. She needed to be sedated. Rather than drive her all the way to my place of work, pretty near 60 miles, I called a friend who had a practice close by, and after supper I took her over.

It didn't take long to repeat the external examination, and take her temperature with a suitably placed thermometer in her behind. Of course we both claimed to know the cause of her pain. She looked a bit bewildered by our clinical debate, so we decided to act rather than discuss the issue. We sedated her.

My use of the plural is a convenient way to mask the fact that when two clinicians work together they sometimes forget who is doing what.

"I saw it first."

"No. I saw it at once"

"You saw the thread. I saw the needle."

"But I pulled it out."

Chuckling at the idiocy of such a banal clinical argument we had meanwhile, one or the other of us, removed a sewing needle deeply embedded in the back of her tongue. The site was swollen and infected, hence the fever. *We* gave her a shot of antibiotic for good measure.

I took her home. I saw the cause at once—a pin cushion and spool of thread on the shelf over her food dish. I was still staring at it when I took the phone call. Somewhat red faced in front of the kids, I pulled the thermometer out.

Dulcie recovered from the incident of her foreign body without any further problem. In a shrewd move we changed the location of the sewing materials. But for a long time, until the girls left home at last, if they wanted to put me in my place, or perhaps distract me when I was beating them at Trivial Pursuit, they would complain of feeling feverish and ask where I kept the thermometer.

22

Shopping at Night

The twilight hours are good times to become acquainted with the world in which we live. ~ John Wanamaker

At one time I was prepared to believe that the phone company programmed my phone to ring at times that their research had shown to be most inconvenient. Possibly disgruntled clients had been recruited to advise them. How else could the phone have rung one evening as two of our teenage daughters, Anne and Jenny, and I, had finished unloading a rented truck and collapsed in mindless heaps amongst the rolled carpets, boxes, and assorted cartons of food strewn across the floor?

That afternoon we had completed a three-hour drive from close to the New Jersey border to upstate New York with about half of our goods and chattels. A change in job; a change in house; a change in schooling for the girls. We had loaded the truck in the morning, moved and unloaded the truck in the afternoon. By the time of the phone call the little hand on the clock nudged eleven. The kids were too exhausted to complain about the TV still waiting to be connected. We had tidied the remains of a nameless takeout dinner into one heap—we hadn't set up a garbage can yet.

The call was from was my wife, Helen. She was still at our old house with the remaining stuff.

"What do I do to get rid of a skunk smell?" She asked, before I had a chance to fire off any unpleasantries. What a time to ask.

"Why now?" I countered.

"Dulcie was skunked in the yard."

Dulcie was our longhaired, tricolor, collie looking type of dog, the former needle-in-the-tongue victim, who was really a spy dog! My wife had brought her from Iran—I think she smuggled her—where she had been rescued by one of the kids as a pup when her mother—the dog's mother—was rounded up in a sweep of the usual canine suspects. I think she worked for the CIA—the dog that is—sniffing out hostile insurgents, but my wife was tight lipped whenever I brought this up, and I couldn't figure out why. Anyway Dulcinea was an Iranian Jube dog—that is Farsi for gutter dog—and she was named for the tragic heroine in Man of La Mancha who also had a gutter history.

This incident occurred before enzyme smell-control shampoos. We still adhered, as did the skunk smell, to the good old standby, tomato juice.

"You need to rub a quart or two of tomato juice into her coat," I said. "Leave it until almost dry, and rinse it out."

I could tell she was thrilled to be told this at 11 pm.

What else could I do? It was a bit like advising a client with an emergency call, but driving back three hours to sniff my own dog seemed a bit out of line. Still my wife had reacted much as a client would; she thought she had been given the brush off.

We three stalwart movers bagged suitable places to sleep, took turns to hog the bathroom and tried to settle into this new environment.

The house we had bought was decorated in early pumpkin. An orange shag carpet dominated the sitting room. We hunkered down, and found that we had bought more than a house. Something that didn't figure in any of the closing statements. We had bought a nest of fleas!

And my wife complained about a poor innocent skunk!

We had each settled in our own way, scratching occasionally, when the phone rang again. Clients who think they have been given the brush off like to harass you.

"Yeah?"

"I got skunked."

"What?"

"When I went out to go to the grocery store for the tomato juice, the skunk was still in the yard. It zapped me as I reached the car."

"My God." I tried to sound as sympathetic and understanding as my sleep and exhaustion-drugged body allowed. "What did you do?" Great opening line, it really impressed her.

"Went to the grocery store."

"And?"

"Everyone was most helpful. I got out pretty quickly."

"They understood about the skunk.?'

"Oh yeah. They understood."

"And when you got home?"

"When I got home I stripped off my jeans in the parking lot and dumped them in the dumpster. Then I bathed Dulcie."

"Good.

"She still stinks."

That was the problem back then, when there was no real solution to the skunk problem.

My daughters and I lived, camped without the guidance and direction of the mummy figure, in our motel-modern pumpkin-flavored house, for a month, scratching, until we could all be reunited under one roof. Dulcinea still had a residual odor, especially noticeable whenever the weather was damp. Fortunately, Helen was odor free—I am sure of that, and I will never change my story.

There were none of the modern flea control preparations then either—pet owners have it so easy nowadays. We battled that problem with three cats and a dog for almost two years. I mean we battled the fleas—the cats and the dog didn't help much.

So should you be part of the phone company

conspiracy and call me late at night about skunks, believe me I do understand the problem. But don't be surprised if I advise an old-fashioned treatment that takes a trip to the grocery store, a messy hour or two to apply, and might leave a reminder of the incident whenever the weather is damp—hopefully, for a couple of years. I might even suggest such a treatment as a cure for fleas. I have to even the score with the phone company some way.

23

The Office Call

I have said it thrice: What I tell you three times is true. ~ *The Hunting of the Snark, Lewis Carroll*

    I took several deep breaths, set my Dale Carnegie smile in place, switched on the inner light and entered the examination room. Mrs. Zigelpush stood on the other side of the examination table, an expression befitting the Captain of the Titanic fixed rigidly on her face. Clutched defiantly to her ample bosom, a scrawny gray cat, in imminent danger of suffocation, gave a muffled howl. I lifted my sagging smile a notch, pinning lip to nose by sheer will power. "How are we today?"

"Fluffy's constipated."

"Ah. Let's take a look then shall *we?*"

    My use of the *royal we* would undoubtedly help Mrs. Zigelpush think that she was included and identify with her unfortunate pet and its problem. The Queen always refers to herself in the plural, a unique and singular use of the number, so I felt justified in borrowing the term for its effect—much like the mastitis drench—as a diagnostic aid. Had I said "Let me take a look," the response I could expect would be no more than a 'Humph.' Now, hopefully, she would participate in the examination, and possibly reveal details of Fluffy's intimate functions more readily than to questions from the impersonal *me*.

    Palpating the wretched animal's abdomen, I peered over my bifocals—acquired recently and worn for effect you understand—and hazarded an historical question.

"Been constipated long?"

"Three days."

"Are you sure?" I am usually careful not to disillusion clients too abruptly. They are quite liable to display an astonishing lack of loyalty, and rush off to the Elsewhere Clinic, leaving behind the bill. One has to try to tell them what they want to hear without being an absolute out-and-out liar. Shades of being a 'trusted magician.'

"Fluffy must be, ah, eliminating somewhere else," I said.

"What?"

"He's pooping somewhere else. Behind the couch or somewhere."

"No, he's not. He's constipated."

"His bowel is quite empty. There's nothing in his tummy."

"Of course," she said, with an air of contempt born of profound knowledge. "That's because he isn't eating."

Patience, patience, I counseled myself. "How long has he not been eating?"

"Ever since he got the bowel blockage," she said, between lips pursed with self assurance.

"What blockage?"

"The one causing his constipation."

"But Mrs. Zigelpush, he doesn't have constipation. His tummy's empty.'"

"That's because he's not been eating."

"How long has..."

I engaged my mind elsewhere, trying to establish a diagnosis. Our voices continued the aimless exchange. The unfortunate Fluffy sneezed. I discerned slight staining at the corners of the nostrils. He coughed and gagged on palpation of his sensitive throat. Ha, a respiratory infection. I opened his mouth. There were ulcerated patches on his tongue from a viral infection. Cats with stuffy noses, sore throats and raw tongues are sometimes reluctant to eat!

I noted in passing we were on our third reprise of the chorus. "Constipated, empty, not eating, blockage. Constipated, empty, not eating, blockage." Memories of childhood jump ropes, double Dutch.

"Fluffy needs medicine," I said, reaching mentally for the antibiotic and the decongestant.

"I know," responded Mrs. Zigelpush, who, determined to see Fluffy restored to his former gluttonous self, now struck for my jugular. "He needs an enema!"

Not to be finessed at this late stage, I pinned up the other side of my lip, and adopted a positive attitude. "This will do the trick." Placing in her hands a bottle of the finest synthetic penicillin and a packet of the finest decongestant pills known to veterinary medicine, I gave her the 'you-were-awfully-smart-to-come-to-me' look.

She read the directions slowly. "What's this?" she said.

"Medicine Mrs. Ziglepush. Medicine. For the whole cat."

"I've never seen an enema given by mouth."

"It's a new technique. Believe me."

Her face cracked for the first time. A vestigial smile twitched the corners of her lips. Fluffy kicked his hind legs, much like a man dying slowly of strangulation. Mrs. Zigelpush clasped him tighter and sailed from the room while thrusting his head ever deeper into the full spinnaker of her bosom.

I unpinned my lips, took a deep breath, licked my forehead, wiped the end of my pen and reached for the patient chart. To one office call, $35. To one office call $35. To one office call, $35. That would cure her cat faster than all the medicine.

24

A Peach of a Case

Making the simple complicated is commonplace; making the complicated simple, awesomely simple, that's creativity. ~ Charles Mingus

"Surgery?!"

My client's eyes widened below the wispy reddish curves that passed for eyebrows and her body trembled like a gigantic Jell-O. Aunt Josephine and I had met for our first professional confrontation—consult.

I knew how she felt. Surgery meant sickness and death! Everyone will tell you that. Her head is filled with medical horror stories—personal experience, or that of a friend, or a friend of a friend's friend—whatever. The horror is always increased in direct proportion to the number of friends in the chain.

I moved out of crushing range, and circled my mental wagons for the verbal attack she was sure to launch as a way of improving my outlook on life.

Aunt Josephine settled her mighty heaving. "Give it to me straight. What are Fidget's chances?"

Holding my jacket lapels I rocked on my heels, looked suitably learned, and deliberated before replying. After all, she should have confidence in her nephew, shouldn't she?

"Come on," she said. "I know an operation is risky. Tell me how risky."

It really is too bad that risk is something owners understand better than clinicians—the possibility of suffering harm or loss—well, at least they have a clear picture of what *they* mean, in their mind. Probably because the word risk comes from the Latin, *resecare*, to cut again, which implies that someone screwed up the first time. To an owner risk is simple—what hope has the animal of surviving the operation!

Now I know, and I'm sure you are aware—because if you are reading this you must be sophisticated, discerning and intelligent—it is not always easy to give a straightforward answer. Clinical judgment is influenced by the owner's wishes. This creates an interesting balance. To a clinician the risk is also complicated by facts, like the severity of the surgery, experience of the surgeon, who's doing the anesthesia, which tech's on duty, and the magical term Physical Status. Physical Status, a scale from 1 to 5 means, in simple terms, what medical shape the pet is in.

Ah, the good old PS! Let's reduce everything to a number that we can say correlates with risk, and then we have something objective to sink our teeth into. We might add a meaningful 'E' if the case is an emergency. However, merely determining this magical number does not help the patient a bit unless we do something, like correct correctable problems and improve improvable functions, but it can justify so much.

First, we can hide behind it. For example we might say, "No problem Mrs. Smith, he checks out as a PS1. That's excellent."

"Ah." Mrs. Smith replies, baffled by the simplicity of veterinary science.

Or perhaps, "I am sorry, he's a PS5E at best, that's the worst possible situation, well-nigh moribund and an emergency to boot, not much hope there, the risk is too great as you can plainly see."

And explaining to the client that one must first determine the pet's physical status helps so much to justify a workup, which hospital policy often demands—sometimes we say that to hide behind because our boss has had a bad day and has threatened to fire anyone who doesn't work-up a patient in a costly way—I mean a proper way!

For every conceivable case we demand data determined by the pet's age and physical condition, and whether or not it presents as an emergency. The older the patient, the more data we demand. We can start with a blood count—count the red and white cells in the blood to make sure there are enough. We might add a serum chemistry profile to uncover underlying problems. Each additional year of age demands more and more investigation—X-rays, EKG, Echocardiogram, Nuclear Magnetic Resonance, skin scan, hair analysis, serum rhubarb levels. Each year we are pressured by peer competition (and our attorneys) to add more sophisticated diagnostic tools. To cover our hindquarters. And to stop insurance rates going through the roof.

"With Fidget," I said to dear Aunt Josephine, "there is a nasty discharge from her private parts, which means her uterus is infected so it really has to come out. And unfortunately she's a bit overweight (I wrote obese in the chart), and she doesn't breathe easily (because she's fat), and her heart's seen better days." I would have tried to pet the little dog to re-assure Auntie, but unfortunately Fidget does not like me, as you will find as my reminiscences unfold, and I did have a vested interest in keeping my fingers intact. I had to rely on a soothing tone of voice. This may have been lost on my relative. She remained silent so I stumbled on.

"She is seven years old, that's middle aged you understand, and she's drinking more and wetting more due to her kidneys not working so hot, so what I'll do is take some blood and run some tests."

"I don't want any of your 'fangled tests,'" said Aunt Josephine, snatching Fidget from the table. She left out the 'new' before the 'fangled tests.' "Why put her through all that, needles and things? Just take all her nature out and get it over."

"I understand." My soothing tone was gone!

Those 'fangled tests,' and 'things,' they'll haunt you every time.

Of course there is always a fallback position, the exception to prove the rule, where the need for immediate surgery overrides the need for a workup. We don't usually talk about this, but we can stretch a point, like if it's one's own pet, or the pet of a moocher who goes from practice to practice with no intention of paying, or if it's Saturday and the lab's closed—or if the client is an Aunt Josephine whom you must stay in good with to figure in her will.

She reminded me of my first fallback position years before.

I was in the staff lounge of a worthy academic establishment, after a late lunch, on the couch, practicing mental isometrics behind closed eyelids, when a client arrived. By taxi. In bathrobe and slippers. And in congestive heart failure. That is, the owner was in congestive heart failure. She had dragged herself from her own sick bed because she wanted Poochie finally fixed before she herself popped off! She told me this. Talk about pressure! Ever the optimist, she kept the taxi waiting, meter running.

So I looked at Poochie.

Poochie was meant to be a Corgi. Ten pounds, ten years old. Intact female. Distended abdomen. Except for a tuft of hair on the top of her head, and on the legs below the elbows and hocks, the dog was a prune—bald, wrinkled and black. She also had a vaginal discharge.

"How long..."

"Six years," my ailing client volunteered—gasped.

My eyebrows, not yet subject to the discipline that comes with years of practice, rose of their own accord.

"Another doctor told me he wanted to spay her," she said. "But, what's spaying have to do with her skin? That's what I say."

Without asking, I had learned that the owner was concerned with the appearance of the skin, not, as Auntie would say, *her nature*.

"And the discharge—how long?"

"Oh she's always had that."

I did not want to precipitate a congestive crisis in the owner. Without waiting to warm hands or stethoscope, super-sleuth launched into a super spiffy exam. Oh my! I could feel abnormal masses in the abdomen. Not the kidneys—ovaries. Ovaries? Like tennis balls! No wonder she had a uterine infection, and skin that mirrored the huge amounts of estrogen coursing through her blood stream.

I called Magic Fingers, and whispered a prayer of thanks for the security of academia. "Do you have a blood count?" he asked. "A chemistry profile? ECG? X-rays? Urinalysis?"

I shook my head at each question. Actually, I am stretching the truth because we didn't have rapid chemistry screens and blood counts in those pre-historic times.

"So what have you got?"

"A Physical Exam," I said proudly.

"In a bald patient with chronic uterine infection, who might also have a wicked hormonal problem, is ten years old and weighs ten pounds?" He appeared to have a surprised tone in his voice.

"And a client in congestive failure, with a taxi waiting," I said. "The meter's still running by the way."

If he had had bi-focals, he would have glared over the top of them.

"If I gas her, will you cut?" I asked innocently.

He delayed briefly in his reply then rose to the challenge. So he ought, he had been teaching surgery since the year dot! Oh, for teamwork. I gave the poor dog a jolt of intravenous fluids and a tad of barbiturate, ventilated with oxygen and a little of the newest anesthetic on the market. Magic Fingers' fingers flew. Piece of cake! Twenty minutes was all it took from decision to operate to recovery, (including the time to commit surgical trespass and take a skin biopsy for the sake of science, you understand). Twenty minutes, and the owner was on her way home, in that waiting taxi, with her pet, happy as a beautician when Aunt Josephine leaves the salon.

The ovaries weighed 10% of the dog's body weight! A bit excessive we both admitted.

Magic Fingers and I didn't know if the client would make it back with her pooch when the stitches were due to come out, but two weeks later we were confounded. They both returned. Both were doing well. When we saw them again three months later even the hair was re-growing—the dog's hair—its little body was covered with soft wispy reddish down, like peach fuzz. The client's congestive failure was controlled. She was fully dressed and wearing shoes. All concerned were amazed, relieved and delighted.

I was remembering all this when my reverie was rudely interrupted by a semi-polite cough from Aunt Josephine. I lifted my gaze to my distant aunt's Corgi colored eyebrows as I lifted Fidget into my arms. "Won't be long Auntie. Take care of it right away." Then, to keep her a little off balance, I glibly added, "You can keep the meter running."

25

A Question of Memory

The man with a clear conscience probably has a poor memory. ~
Author unknown.

    The gentleman stood on the far side of the examination table, a grin borrowed straight from the Cheshire cat dividing his gnomic face, and what I should have recognized as a devilish twinkle in his eye. The white dog collar, in striking contrast to his sober black suit, cut deep into his neck below a pair of matched chins. It gave the first clue to his origins. But the voice it was that did it. A melodic lilt that told of his birth under the sign of the leprechaun.
    I greeted him.
    "Ah, for sure, and isn't it the beautiful mornin' indeed," he replied.
    At his side, a Boxer, all slobber-and-twist, put its forefeet on the examination room table and spread great globs of saliva in an urgent display of affection.
    "What seems to be the problem, Father?"
    My receptionist, obviously entranced by the fresh breath of Irish blarney so early in the morning, had quite forgotten to write anything of value on the record card, except 'Reverend.' A whispered query to her as I approached the examination room had been met with a smile and an enigmatic shrug.
    "Well, you see, and isn't he drinking his terrible fill of the water now."

Between us, we wrangled the dog onto the table, and as he flexed and wiggled his hinged body I began to examine him—at least those portions that remained still long enough.

"How long has he been doing that?"

"That's a hard question for sure," he answered. "I can't rightly remember."

"A week? A month?"

"Now there you have me Doctor. You do indeed. But I'll make sure to watch if he continues."

I resumed the examination. This would probably be the healthiest dog to brave the clinic all day.

"Did it start suddenly, or has his drinking been creeping up gradually?"

"Oh, he's always been a good drinker that he has, though like most of us, there's likely a little of the gradualism too, no doubt." He winked.

"Meaning" I asked.

"That I forget." His head tilted down so that the twinkling eyes, shy for the moment, peered up from under shaggy brows.

"How much does he drink?" I asked.

"Ah sure, and isn't it the plurality of gallons."

"The what?"

"The plurality of gallons surely. Two, three at least, maybe more."

"Have you measured how much?"

"Now, didn't I forget to remember to do that?"

With the physical examination completed, we lifted the dog to the floor. I had not made a single significant finding, so I returned to questioning my delightful client.

"Do you have to fill his bowl frequently?" I asked.

"His bowl? I don't remember whether he has a bowl."

"What does he drink out of?"

"Out of? I've always turned on the faucet you see. Doesn't he drink his fill now from the flowing stream, so he does."

"Father," I said, retrieving my pen as it began a potentially hazardous journey through the Boxer's digestive tract. "Your dog appears to be in fine shape. What I want you to do is make sure that for the next week he drinks from a bowl. And please record the number of bowls. Can you remember to do that?"

"Remember that? Doctor what do you take me for? Of course I'll remember. Sure and isn't it a poor memory that only works backwards?"

I escorted him to the waiting room and left him at the front desk. As I walked away I heard him charming my receptionist.

"Now, about the small matter of the fee," he said.

"Oh, that's quite all right, Father." I waited for the punch line. She had a reverence for Reverends, something about insurance in the afterlife.

"The Doctor said to forget all charges."

26

The Tartan Coat Syndrome

Sometimes it helps to look for the obvious. ~ Thomas Magnum,
Magnum P.I.

    I hung my jacket on a coat hook, tried to button my white coat over an early-developing mid-life bulge and entered the examination room. My nemesis waited. This time Mrs. Ziglepush was not suffocating her scrawny cat, Fluffy. She had brought her unfortunate dog, Snookums, instead. A designer mutt of indeterminate pedigree about whom everything was *medium*—medium length coat, beneath which he was hidden, white, with medium sized black blotches, or vice-versa, medium length muzzle and mid-brown eyes. The ears were not quite floppy, not quite pricked.
    Mrs. Ziglepush was my first truly two-faced client. When she entered the exam room, weighed down with the burden of Snookum's or Fluffy's latest near-death experiences, everything about her face drooped; eyelids, cheeks, lips and jowl. Even her ears were weighted down with age-inappropriate golden hoops—the brightest thing about her. When she left, whether or not her pet was on the road to recovery, but more likely because I hadn't made it noticeably worse, she stood a good two inches taller. Everything about her face, reached, as if in gratitude, towards heaven. Her cheeks had tightened, gone any hint of sagging flesh. Her eyes, wide open, glowed brightly beneath the positive upward curl of her eyebrows. Her dullest

feature—the age-inappropriate ear rings.

Despite her pessimism when she arrived at the office, she always lifted my spirits, because, no matter what I did, or didn't do, she left radiating good cheer.

"Oh Doctor," Mrs. Zigelpush cried. Her eyes, underscored by multiple dark rings that would make Saturn envious, drooped like a Basset's ears—there didn't I tell you. "Snookums keeps itch, itch, itch, all the time. He keeps me awake nights. Mr. Zigelpush wants us to sleep in another room."

I selected an attitude of patient understanding. The office visit fee included one mildly sympathetic smile, and at least two positive comments on how perceptive she appeared to be about Snookums' problems.

"Home is the place where you can scratch where you itch." (Occasional light humor is included in the office fee). I rubbed the mutt behind the ears. It curled its lips. Perhaps it learned it from Fidget. Mrs. Zigelipush's eye-lids drooped further.

"How long has he been scratching?"

"Since last summer." It was then early January.

I peered at his shining coat, and ran my fingers through hair so soft Mrs. Zigelpush should be making a fortune from TV shampoo commercials. A delicate aroma of mint and wild honey wafted through the examination room. Apart from slight thinning of the coat along the back, perhaps a mild reddening of the skin above the tail, there was absolutely nothing to see. Nixville.

"His coat is beautifully clean," I observed.

"He had his bath this morning, didn't you, Snookums." The dog licked her face, no doubt delighted that the flea dirt, skin scales, dander and any other clinical evidence of his unsavory condition were washed away before I had a chance to see it. I shuddered. I have a thing about dog's licking faces. I know, I know, almost every pet owner allows it. But, no matter how I try, I cannot forget that dogs use their tongues as toilet paper.

I ground my teeth in frustration at Snookums' appearance. This was the second case today of an owner tampering with the evidence. The first had thoroughly scrubbed her cat's ears thus removing all visible cause for its interminable head shaking.

Evidence!

Then I remembered Heidi.

Heidi was a well-fed Dachshund, and I a mere intern when we met, still unsure which end of the stethoscope went where. Heidi's owner had stepped out of a 1920s clothing catalog. As different in appearance as she could possibly be from my aunt or Mrs. Ziglepush. Where their appearance might be described as generous, Heidi's owner was tall and slender, her height exaggerated by a similar shaped face, a soft hat pulled down over her ears, and a dress than hung almost to the ground. Her concern for her pet was palpable. After all I was the sixth veterinarian to be challenged by Heidi's unique syndrome and, as I was to discover, her own problem.

Heidi had spells. She froze up. She stalled, balked, stopped. Quite unpredictably, while out walking, the little dog would come to a sudden halt, unable to place one foot in front of the other.

Starting in late fall, the condition had persisted through the winter.

I launched into the examination sequence programmed into me by a succession of experienced clinicians, ever hopeful that I would some day possess enough smarts to be able to earn a living on my own as a veterinarian.

The general physical exam was unrewarding. Apart from a well-padded body, Heidi's systems appeared—as we say—within normal limits. A specialized orthopedic exam of all her legs and joints yielded nothing. An intense neurological scrutiny failed to reveal a problem with her nervous system. I ran a rapid urine test for something to do. This added to the confusion of normality. Radiography drew a blank. In keeping with five previous veterinarians, I was at a loss.

All my learning, all my studying, all my confidence, and I was at a loss. It was extremely humbling.

With great patience, I thought, for a new graduate, I explained each step, each probe and each clinical finding. At my confession of failure she did an imitation of a tragic swoon. This was more than a poor intern had been trained for. The clinic function ground to a halt. With the aid of older colleagues, she was comforted, reassured, promised a further referral, given a re-check appointment and steered toward the door.

Out of curiosity, from a convenient window, my colleagues and I watched with perplexed fascination as the strange client lead her puzzling pooch across the street. Between steering her to the door and our surreptitious observation, the owner had evidently contrived to fit Heidi into a doggy-coat, a splendid garment in Royal Stuart tartan colors. It stretched from her ears to her tail, and hung down her sides to scrape the ground. Much like her owner's dress.

Suddenly Heidi trod on it with a hind foot. She seized up, stalled, balked, stopped. With her paw firmly on her own coat tails she was unable to move a step. Her long body wiggled with the ineffectual effort of moving one foot after the next. The owner stood mute watching her poor pet, then bent down and comforted the beast by stroking its head.

At last Heidi lifted the correct foot, moved it off the coat, stepped forward boldly and resumed the waddling gait characteristic of the plumper members of her breed. The mystery disease was solved—the cure, shorten the hem of Heidi's coat,

Someone hastily chased after the pair to deliver the diagnosis and treatment, barely beating the client to the local bus, at that moment drawing to the curb.

Mrs. Zigelpush coughed politely focusing my attention on the current case. "So, what is Snookums' problem, Doctor?"

I beamed at them both. "Snookums has a bad case of Tartan Coat Syndrome," I said.

"Oh. Something's wrong with her coat? Is it serious?"

"It could be. What a good thing you brought her in. We call Snookums' problem an *occult* condition," I told her. "One that exists, but can't always be seen."

I scribbled orders for a suitable anti-itch medication and advised the use of a flea control product for all her pets. "They're going around this year," I said and gave her the printed handout on seasonal allergies, handed the case notes to the nurse, and dispatched Mrs. Zigelpush to the front desk.

Thank you, Heidi! Taking my jacket from the coat hook, I tripped out to lunch.

27

"You Know…"

*"The time has come," the Walrus said, "To talk of many things": ~
Through the Looking Glass, Lewis Carroll*

"Tell him, Mom."
"It's your dog."
Mother and daughter looked at one another.
"But… you know."
I stood bewildered.

Usually I knew why someone visited the office. I had been known, with a rare flash of brilliance, to actually read the case notes before I went into an examination room. On this chart the receptionist had written Examination. So informative. As I headed for the exam room I had asked her what this couple was here for. She had smiled. Whatever it was, neither client wanted to tell me either.

There is really only one subject that does that to people. Reproduction, or sex if you can't spell the long version.

So much of veterinary medicine deals with the fundamentals of life. Many days I feel that our entire existence revolves around bodily fluids. That's Darwin's fault. He showed that with time animals adapt to survive. Reproduction allows the minute changes in each generation to add up, eventually producing a recognizable change. So it all comes down to sex. And we veterinarians don't help. What do we do? We focus much of our attention on spaying and neutering, in a feeble attempt to control the results of urges that millions of years have bred into every species.

I ran the possibilities through my head. This might be a neuter candidate. Even from behind an examination table I could see his proud carriage advertising his undoubted male gender.

I adopted an inquisitive expression.

They looked at each other, the daughter's mouth open in exasperation, and probably in horror that she might have to be the one to tell me.

"Mom!"

"It's a…" Mom said. "You see…"

Frequently the embarrassment is on our side of the table. In this age of political correctness one must be careful what questions to ask, and how to ask them. I should have had a nurse with me for back up. I usually did, but on that day we were stretched a bit thin. I was on my own.

This time *they* were embarrassed. I knew how it felt—been there.

My first embarrassing gender moment happened when I was an intern, the lowest on the clinical totem pole, striving to appear so calm, collected, and in control. The client was in her twenties, holding her pooch on the exam table. I stood across from her going into my routine of veterinary super sleuth—peering in its ears, checking teeth and gums, palpating, prodding—when she took off her jacket. I carried on. As I focused on her puppy I saw her, out of the corner of my eye, unbutton her cardigan. She threw it on the floor. Then her fingers started a struggle with her blouse buttons.

This I had not been trained for. What should I do?

I continued as if nothing strange were happening. Of course it is absolutely normal for your attractive female clients to undress in front of their doctor—but their veterinarian? At the same time fingers of stress caressed my spine like cold needles as half of my mind wondered where this was going.

I decided to face it head on. I looked directly at her.

Her expression was blank. Her face pale. "It's hot in here," she said, as she prepared to slip out of her blouse.

Almost too late I understood. Letting her pooch decide its own fate I nipped smartly around the table. I caught her as she fainted.

Luckily I didn't need to do CPR. That's when I noticed I was sweating—it must have been from the heat of course. If I remember right she was a most attractive young lady. (Now isn't that polite?) I adroitly summoned a receptionist of a similar gender to help. She told me later the poor girl had no recollection of the incident. It appears her mind shut down before the imminent collapse of her body.

Neither her dog, nor any other in the clinic, was harmed in the episode or the reporting thereof.

But here I was, mired in the present, practicing under completely new rules where conduct is determined by political correctness. I was without a technician or nurse and must handle any embarrassment, on either side, as best I could, with the experience of years of red faces under my belt.

"There's a lump," mother said. "You know. Underneath."

A clinical clue! The 'you know, underneath' routine is a giveaway.

"How long?" I asked.

"It comes and goes."

"Can you show me where?"

Maintaining a discrete distance form the offending pathology she pointed to the middle of the sheath.

"And it comes and goes?"

"Yes."

Now was the moment of truth.

"He's an adolescent pup," I said. "He is having a partial erection."

They looked at me as if I had stepped out of an MTV video.

"It's what?" mother said, rather loudly.

They looked at each other, vying for whose eyebrows could rise higher.

"I didn't know," mother said, as I watched a pink flush of embarrassment light up her cheeks.

"Mom!" said her daughter, an expression of complete surprise on her face. "How did you ever have me?"

28

The Silence of the Hams

The dramatist only wants more liberties than he can really take. ~
Henry James

"Your aunt is in the waiting room." The receptionist skipped away before I could ask if she had her little dog, Fidget, with her.

Fidget's successful surgery a month or two before had brought mixed blessings. Aunt Josephine had been ecstatic to the point of grunting that I must know my job. "At least you didn't lose her," she said.

Everyone should have an Aunt Josephine, if for no other reason than to keep them humble. Anyway why should I suffer alone?

"There must be something about you," Auntie had observed about ten days after the magical event while I was trying to remove the stitches. She narrowed her eyes to thin slits—Auntie that is. "She only yaps at you."

Quite. But she had still brought Fidget to me, not taken her to someone else. Perhaps it was the family rate she was charged, whatever. I had held my own counsel, even hazarded a smile.

"You see," she reminded me, which she now did whenever she saw me, "You didn't need "those *fangled tests* and things."

"New, Auntie," I said. "New fangled."

"Dreadful things! Needles." She shuddered. (Maybe this was a weakness I could someday exploit. I filed the sight of her shudder away.)

Fidget's yapping had been one of the diagnostic criteria in Fidget's illness. She didn't yap at me in my office the morning that Auntie had brought her in, a truer sign of the seriousness and severity of her condition than any test. So she had been rushed into surgery despite Auntie's conviction that she would never see her again, so slim were her chances. She didn't add *with you*, but I caught the tone, hidden, like her slitted eyes, behind thin lips. Did I say that right? Auntie often muddles me.

Anyway about the mixed blessings I mentioned earlier, unfortunately they brought Auntie to the clinic door rather more frequently than before, but her visits did give me hope for that being-in-her-will thing, in case she might want to leave me a bequest in Fidget's name.

I slunk into the waiting room.

"There you are," she boomed over her heaving bosom, swollen further with the ten-pound canine bundle firmly clasped to her.

"How's Fidget?" I asked.

She ignored the question. "I hear you are in a play or something."

She never ceases to surprise me. Her opening salvo rendered me quite inarticulate for a moment or two. Not a state I am used to.

"It's a small role for the local community theater," I stuttered.

"So, why are you in it?"

Where does one start? But she let me off the hook; she didn't wait for an answer.

"What," she said, "Is the possible connection between clinicians, so-called?" I waited for the end of the sentence. Like a newscaster, after a pause for dramatic effect, and also to hitch up her bra so she could breathe, Auntie continued, "and actors?"

With Auntie, silence is often more prudent than argument. So this ham tried to remain quiet about his true thespian calling. But my charge through a succession of bit-parts to leading man, with this theater group had been, in my humble view, quite meteoric, and my enthusiasm overcame caution

"Well, the two professions are always on stage, performing for their public, dramatizing a role, standing in the limelight of public scrutiny," I said, throwing caution to the winds. I did not mention the yearning for stardom that gnawed like a great parasitic worm within me. That's a veterinary allusion.

Aunt Josephine has given me, many times over the years, the uncensored benefit of her wisdom. I felt a benefit coming. When I had told her, years before, that I had done a residency in anesthesia at a medical school, the honor of being accepted into a medical school program washed over her like a dying flood light sweeping the stage.

"Anesthetists," she announced, "are failed surgeons!"

And when I once, in a moment of serious inattention, told her that I intended to write for publication, she proclaimed that in her view writers wrote about things because they couldn't do them!

Opinions, she often stated, should be the sole prerogative of those who understood the facts. In her world that is a limited range of individuals. But despite her censorial attitude, her honesty to her own opinions was in a way quite refreshing, so confident was she as she gamely bore her cross through life, her cross to discern and wildly publicize the truth about—whatever.

I certainly have met others whom have pointed me forward with advice or comment, my Anatomy Professor for example.

The half-way point in my veterinary course included an enormously important examination in anatomy. In our classical approach to animal disease we studied assiduously the various species, starting with the horse (I told you it was classical) from whence all bodily form originated. Then we compared the anatomy, and the organs of cow, sheep, dog and pig to the aforementioned horse. Cats may have been mentioned somewhere. Anyway, this was before vaccinations against the common childhood disorders were readily available, (for students, not horse, cow, sheep or pig—even cat.) So in accordance with Murphy's Law, I contracted measles a scant three weeks before the exam. With a borrowed microscope tucked under my arm I closeted myself in my digs and lived on baked beans and other delights that my girlfriend brought while I attempted to cram for the exam. Alas. The eyes swelled, fever and headaches took their toll and I did little studying.

About a week before the exam I returned to college, slightly anxious (blue funky panic) about my chances of successfully negotiating this somber hurdle. As we had no advisors or counselors in those days, I took my qualms to the Prof. To him I expressed my concern. He nodded sagely and decided I needed a tonic to boost my physical status. He carefully wrote out a prescription to be taken to Ewan Thomas, the local apothecary, and sealed it in an official college envelope.

As I left his office I must have been recovered sufficiently to notice the twinkle in his eye. Before I paid a call on the said Mr. Thomas I pried open the missive.

Recipe: (This means "Take Thou) "Bigger Bloody Fools than I have passed this examination."

Sig: To be read three times a day until March 21st.

It was signed with his name and a list of degrees that filled the rest of the line.

Whilst it was not quite the tonic I had hoped for, the advice conjured up a smile to brighten my worry-wracked face. However, it had come at the expense of a serious error on my part. The Professor now knew my name.

We bumped into each other again in the hallway a few months later. Actually, we were passing in the hallway, when he held up his hand to stop me. I thought he was about to enquire about my health or my tonic.

"Heard you rode a horse in the circus," he said.

Oops!

On pain of severe disciplinary action students were not allowed to indulge in any activity that might reflect poorly on the college. His voice was non-committal. I did not know if he thought that by riding a circus horse I had made a spectacle of myself in public? I didn't think so, but others, even sweet Aunt Josephine might disagree. But I couldn't deny it, I had ridden a horse in the circus.

"Yes, Sir," I said.

On a recent trip to the circus I had witnessed a brilliant display of acrobatics, *voltage*, on a bareback horse, by a Hungarian troupe. Then the Ringmaster issued a challenge to the crowd, "Come try."

What's the Hungarian for idiot? Allow me to admit that I am one idiot who tried. The only one, actually.

While I stood sheepishly across the ring from the large horse, a clown tied a safety belt around my waist from which a rope looped up into the heights of the big top and back to two more clowns charged with ensuring my survival. My instructions were to run across the ring and jump onto the horse's back.

Never have I seen anything grow so big, so quickly, as I stumbled across the sawdust.

I jumped.

I crashed full into the side of an animal the size of the wooden model the Greeks gave to Troy.

The crowd cheered, convinced that I was a plant employed by the circus.

Reaching high above me, I managed to reach the brute's withers. I attempted to jump. That was equally ludicrous. Then the clowns took my weight on the rope and pulled in time to my bounces. Soon I was hurtling upwards, way past the top of the horse. This, too, the crowd sensed was part of the show. Then, with the clowns juggling my weight, and me grasping for the mane, I landed on an equine back broader than any taught in anatomy.

We set off at a gentle canter. The ringmaster took time to intersperse his monologue to the crowd with instructions to me.

First time around the ring, sit. That was fine with me.

Second time around the ring, kneel. This was easier than you might think because the back was so wide.

Third time, stand.

I stood. This was so exhilarating. My first time in the spotlight. Not knowing that this simple act was sowing the seeds of future cravings for the limelight, floodlights, spotlights, footlights—I am carried away sometimes.

We cantered completely around the ring. Damn, I was good. I was standing on a bareback horse! And I had an audience loving it. Loving my performance!

The circus ring had an entrance where the low wall can be opened to let performers in and out. It was of course closed for this, my debut public performance. As we approached it on the third circuit the horse checked her gait ever so slightly. It disturbed my balance, ever so slightly. To recover I took a couple of paces forward toward the huge shoulders surging in rhythmic motion with every stride, ever so slightly.

Oops!

I was not going to recover. Even ever so slightly!

I launched myself into space, trusting the good folk on the end of the rope. Taken by surprise they were a millisecond or two behind my flight. I swooped low over the sawdust. The Ringmaster flung himself to the ground. I soared over the crowd, then back over the ring. The crowd cheered.

A few more swings, each shorter than the last, then I was back standing in the ring. The harness was removed. I waved to the crowd, bowed in several directions, like tournament tennis players do now—they probably copied it from me. This was my first curtain call.

Now the Prof stood before me in the hallway asking me about it. The pucker factor was on a steep rise. He nodded sagely.

"Jolly good show. More students should involve themselves like that."

I don't usually drop my jaw, but on that occasion, stooping to pick it up, I could only smile at the quirks of human nature. Then I recalled that he insisted that students request a day off on the first Wednesday in June to go to the Epsom Derby, one of the jewels of the English Triple Crown of horse racing. He was most certainly 'Of the students, by the students, for the students!'

Aunt Josephine coughed, or rather made a pay attention type noise.

"I hear you take off all your clothes on the stage!"

Dramatic license provides broad scope for exhibitionism. I thought I had performed brilliantly in my short acting career. A couple of musicals, bit parts here and there in professional productions, and a dramatic rise in our local theater from butler, to West End Producer, to a semi-nude scene—all in a mere 18 months. Next stop People Magazine and Entertainment Tonight!

"Not quite, Auntie. Not all of them."

My euphoria at her recognition of my Thespian calling suddenly took a hit. I felt the tell-tale feeling of blood draining from the face. Now I was waiting for the summation, judgment and sentence, from Aunt Josephine.

"I don't take them off completely, Auntie, honest." I stammered.

"Humph."

"The play calls for it..." Lame response, keep quiet you fool.

"Humph," she repeated. She stared at me for several seconds, imagining the obvious, no doubt. I squirmed under her gaze.

"Good show. Good show. Didn't think you had the balls."

She never ceased to surprise me.

29

A Weighty Issue

If you have much, give of your wealth; if you have little, give of your heart. ~ Arabian Proverb

"I forgot what I'm supposed to remember, so I made this appointment to re-acquaint meself with your kind instructions." My favorite Reverend's eyes twinkled under his bushy brows as brightly as on the day we had met, two short weeks before. On that occasion he had presented his all-slobber-and-twist Boxer because he was, in the Reverend's own words "Drinking the plurality of gallons, so he is."

His chins bulged against the restraint of his clerical collar and bobbed in time to his gentle Irish lilt. There was no sign of his dog. He stood quite alone, a small, wrinkled, ordained, Irish copy of Friar Tuck.

"If the truth be said, Sister Agnes made the appointment for me, so she did, her memory being better than mine, because I knew that if she remembered then she wouldn't forget if I remembered to ask her what it was I had forgotten."

"Ah, yes," I said, unraveling his words as I remembered his parting line at his last visit. "Of course I'll remember," he'd said. "Sure and isn't it a poor memory that only works backwards?"

"And you remembered?" I couldn't resist asking.

"Surely, there you have me. Didn't the good sister write it in her grocery list for the week? We are listed with

Friday's fish order."

"So she would remember to tell you?"

"So she wouldn't forget."

"So now you expect me to remember what I said?"

He grinned. "I know that yourself, like Sister Agnes, remembered to write it down, because I seem to recall that you did."

"So I did." Careful, I was beginning to lapse into his magical pattern of speech. "So that's all you need? The instructions?" I asked.

"To reacquaint myself, yes."

He had presented his exuberant Boxer a week or two before because he suspected the dog drank too much, a diagnostic challenge, because, not only was the dog in wondrous health, so he was—I was starting to think his way too—he drank from a flowing faucet, so he did.

We could probably have done this quite easily over the telephone, but when I thought of following the rhythmical language gymnastics that flowed so easily off his tongue, I mentally thanked my guardian angel for this closer encounter.

I scanned my notes. "So is he still drinking—the plurality of gallons?"

"Ah yes, he has a good thirst. So that's what we were here then, for sure. I think."

"And have you been counting the number of bowls he drinks a day?"

"His bowls?"

"You were to only let him drink from a bowl, not the running water."

"Now I remember why I came. Thank you, Doctor. I'll have Sister Agnes to write it down for me."

He could be forgiven for his lapses. He had been retired years longer than I had been in practice, and lived with his dog, on a modest church stipend, in a small apartment behind the church hall.

"So you haven't measured what he drinks."

"That's something I have still to do."

"Perhaps I should write it down for you. So you won't forget to tell her."

"Sure and that won't be necessary. Isn't she in the waiting room this very minute, so she is."

Sister Agnes sat in the corner reading. Two seats away from her a Boxer, leashed to a chair, threatened to pull the seat from its attachment to the wall.

"I didn't realize you had him with you," I said.

"Sure and isn't he not mine."

"Not yours?"

"No, Sir. Isn't he another dog entirely."

"He sure looks like him. Correction—she looks like him." The twin of the Reverend's dog strained and twisted her joyful body at the end of the leash, dispensing saliva and happiness in equal measure. She gyrated to a strange background sound. An unfamiliar rhythm, as if accompanied by her own, subdued, Mariachi band.

"Now, would I forget my own dog?"

Before I could comment, Sister Agnes volunteered that the owner had stepped out to his car for a moment. It was wondrous easy to follow her speech, so it was. Watch it! As I glanced out of the window in search of the owner, a beat up station wagon stuttered and backfired out of the parking lot.

We looked at each other, each in turn peered at the dog, then, as one, turned to the receptionist, June. She stared back at us, tossed her head and shrugged.

"He left this on the counter," she said, waving an envelope at us. "It says Doctor on the front."

The envelope hid a written note, lying in wait for an unwary doctor, and a small amount of money. "Jessie has been vomiting for three days. Fix her and find her a home." That was short and to the point. A note as sparse as the Reverend's memory.

"Ah, the trusting nature of the man," said Father.

It reminded me of other times when animals had been

left. Litters of kittens had been found, on occasion, boxed, motherless and mewling on our clinic doorstep. They were usually noteless. As a student I had once found a dog chained to the college gate. Also noteless. But the one I remembered most clearly was a litter of German shepherd puppies, left in a litter bin outside a supermarket.

They arrived at the clinic one morning, one by one, each rescued by a prospective new owner, every one of whom, heaping invective on the cruel, heartless, cold, devil who had thus abandoned such a beautiful litter, steadfastly refusing to relinquish their newly adopted pet. They formed a loose-knit club, and agreed amongst themselves to book appointments for shots and worm medicine on the same day. I saw most of them regularly until they had completed their puppy vaccinations. Being a softy, I gave them a group discount.

My reverie was interrupted by the arrival of my technician, summoned hastily by June, before I had the temerity, cruelty or stupidity, to call the shelter about the boxer left in our clinic. "What do you want me to do with her?" The tone of her voice implied I had little choice.

"Bring her in the back," I sighed. Jessie wiggled past to an intriguing metallic beat.

"Ah Doctor, it is a Christian man you are, for sure." Father's spiritual approval sealed both our fates, Jessie's and mine.

On examination something felt strange in the most forward part of Jessie's abdomen. I had merely to mention it for my tech to plunge her arms through the shoulder straps of a lead lined apron and lead her into the X-ray room.

Jessie's stomach held five huge ball bearings.

I didn't stand a chance. In fact my people, watched over by my new spiritual guide, had already opened a surgery pack, readied the anesthetic machine, and were placing an intravenous catheter, while I still studied the radiograph in amused disbelief.

The surgery was remarkably uneventful. I confirmed that she had been spayed, and except for some bruising of the stomach wall, an area I was able to avoid at surgery, the rest of her innards looked none the worse for their metallic massage as Jessie had wriggled her way through the last few days. The ball bearings weighed a pound each. I have read of stranger foreign bodies retrieved from dogs anxious to challenge their digestive tracts, but never anything as heavy.

Jessie recovered completely. Aided by the lack of an overactive imagination, unlike Mrs. Ziglepush or Aunt Josephine, the patient did not appreciate that she was considered ill, had withstood surgical assault and should act in a manner appropriate to an invalid. By next morning she slobbered and twisted her greetings to anyone passing her cage, trying to share with all, her love of life.

Her brief convalescence was clouded by the unspoken thoughts of what to do with her. Like me, my staff already cared to the limit for the waifs and strays whose plight and charms they had been unable to resist.

Our problem was solved unexpectedly by a return visit from the Reverend. Sister Agnes trailed a pace behind. I thought it would have been safer for her to lead, as she remembered the way and acted as his chauffeur.

"Didn't I forget to ask you," he began. Here we went again.

"What is it this time?"

"Sister Agnes kindly reminded me to ask you where you intended to send the dog."

"I wasn't going to refer him anywhere. Not until you count the bowls he drinks.

"No, no. Not my dog. Jessie."

He brought them both with him when the stitches were to be removed, arriving in a flurry of dogs and leashes, each one trying to be the first to dislocate an arm. He crossed the parking lot at a trot, dignified but faster than his usual, more measured, tread. Sister Agnes trailed behind in a swirl of habit. Straining to hold his own in an unmatched contest, his feet hit the ground firmly at every step, bouncing his chins in cadence with his stride.

I wanted to tell him what a wondrous thing he had done, so he had, but he forestalled me.

"A mighty dog," he said. "A mighty dog. Sister Agnes reminded me that Jessie proves the proverb, so she does, her being neglected, ill, abandoned, and no one to pay for her treatment."

"And what is that?"

"Oh surely you remember now? Isn't it 'the harder you fall, the higher you bounce'."

Like his chins.

30

Two Ladies of Girth

Ex unitate vires—from unity, strength.

"You have two walk-ins." June squinted at me, holding two case records up to her face. She was hiding something besides her smile.

I poked my head into the waiting room.

"Fluffy's too quiet."

"Fidget is sick!"

Two ladies spoke at once. The day I had long dreaded had arrived, Aunt Josephine and Mrs. Ziglepush, in the office, together. Was there no mercy?

It was, of course, inevitable that they would meet one day, particularly since my heroic efforts on behalf of Auntie's little mutt, Fidget, now brought her to the office more frequently. And Mrs. Ziglepush was apt to drop in unannounced at any time with Fluffy who, still scrawny, persisted in continuing to develop syndromes and symptoms to satisfy every carefully hidden care-giving bone in Mrs. Ziglepush's ample body.

I recoiled through the door, the better to gather my breath and wits.

There were such similarities between the two owners, not only limited to their physical shape, although Auntie's equatorial girth was a little lower. They both knew their pet's diagnosis and its cause before arriving at the office, which they visited merely to confirm their certainties. They both nodded, and went ah-ha in the same doubting tone. I think they both rolled their eyes in the same direction. And they were both careful to keep their checkbooks hidden.

Fidget and Fluffy were however as different as their owners were similar. Fluffy, the cat, was scrawny, defiant, and always in imminent danger, in the office at least, of being suffocated by his generously built owner. Little Fidget, plump as ever, appeared red eyed as usual. This I attributed to her fierce yapping which she did whenever she saw me, me alone, no one else you understand. Of the two, I think Fluffy liked me most. Possibly because when I held or examined him, he could at least breathe. Fidget, on the other hand, had never forgiven me for some slight or indiscretion that I had apparently committed, to which she had taken immediate and permanent offence. If I muddle the motives of owners and pets from time to time, I can only offer as defense, that in their presence, I am really sometimes confused.

In the hallway I had been through my emergency routine to control hyperventilation, straightened my stethoscope around my neck, lined up the pens in my pocket and smoothed imaginary creases from my jacket. I walked out to greet them.

With both ladies present, the waiting room was filled to capacity. Their bodies, attitudes and pets left no room for anything or anyone. And of course, with both dropping in, there was some competition about who should be seen first.

Events developed quickly. Fidget started yapping. Gripping Fluffy tightly, Mrs. Ziglepush yelled at her to be quiet so *she* could be heard. Fidget rolled over and peed. Mrs. Ziglepush skidded on the puddle and sat heavily in one of the strategically located chairs, squeezing Fluffy, who yowled, setting up even more furious yapping from Fidget. While Mrs. Ziglepush fought to regain her composure my aunt spoke. "See?" That's all she said. "See?"

"See what?" I asked.

"She yaps at you, and now look what you've done." I didn't see what I had done, but some things are a matter of opinion. Mrs. Ziglepush understood. She immediately transferred her ire from Fidget to me.

"You see," she said, not to be outdone.

I felt like yelling, "Code yellow in aisle four," but refrained out of courtesy. My technician, June, bless her heart, earned a future bonus by springing to my defense and assisting Mrs. Ziglepush. If that lady had ruffled feathers, they would soon be preened and primped by June's attentions. She gave June a wan smile. Fluffy wriggled out of her arms and hid under the chair.

That left Auntie.

"I knew Fidget was sick," she said. "She must have a bladder infection."

"I think she was scared, Auntie," I said.

"Nonsense, she would never do that." Unfortunately she would, but now was not the time to argue. Fidget had taken a long time to grow out of the unfortunate submissive wetting stage when she was younger. She would still do it when frightened.

Fidget had always been a submissive dog except when she was yapping at me. It nearly cost me dearly. Come to think of it, that was probably where my imagined slight to Fidget's psyche had occurred. Isn't it strange what rekindles a memory?

A few years previously, some time before Fidget's uterine infection, Auntie had wanted her living room floor coated with polyurethane. I had been chosen as most likely to succeed in doing the floor. This was in the days when it was still in a smelly mineral base, not the ecologically acceptable water based floor stuff that is available now. Polyurethane, once applied, is sticky until it dries. That takes time. I had barely completed the Herculean task when Fidget appeared. Auntie had left me alone to do the floor and had assured me that Fidget was confined. She had been merely hiding. She trotted boldly onto the newly treated floor.

Aagh!

She examined the stuff clinging to her paws and looked to be about to sit down to investigate them further. I dared not yell at her. Yelling would have made her roll on her back and pee. I daren't imagine it. Fidget, covered in goo, impossible to clean off. Fidget shaved. Auntie's ire.

Lying through my teeth, murmuring sweet nothings about a cookie, I offered my hand towards her. Anyway, I had chosen the right word. Fidget came over to me, leaving little poly pad marks on the hall carpet. I closed the living room door behind her. I leaned against the door jamb and muttered, "Stupid dog." She rolled on the carpet and peed!

I wondered where she had learned the word stupid. Auntie never revealed that secret.

I scrubbed at the paw marks on the carpet. I scrubbed at the pee. I used most of Auntie's paper towels drying the mess, and then had to vacuum up the paper fuzz that clung to every place I had scrubbed.

Somehow I removed the paw marks. So I kept quiet about those. The pee patch was still damp when Auntie arrived home. I told her about that. I hoped she wouldn't notice the paw prints on the newly treated floor. If she did, she never said. But when she examined the damp patch where Fidget had had her little submissive fit, she glared at me, and scooped her up.

"What did you do to her?" she said in a stunningly loud voice. I held my breath lest Fidget repeat her indiscretion in her owner's arms. Luckily her bladder was empty, but Fidget picked up on the querulous tone and henceforth blamed me for what she must have thought was a scolding. She started to yap at me. Now she did it every time we met.

June was mopping the clinic floor. I didn't think I had included that in her job description, but she knew on which side her bread was buttered. She slipped a urine test strip in the puddle before she cleared it away—veterinary receptionists being, of necessity, awfully versatile. Mrs.

Ziglepush continued to glare, but had to relent somewhat when Fluffy rubbed himself against my legs, as cats do. He, at least, was happy. Nevertheless she had to takes sides, so she chose Auntie's.

"Of course she has a bladder infection," Mrs. Ziglepush said vehemently, nodding to Auntie, "Anyone can see that."

Their "humphs" were in unison.

"Why is Fluffy here?" I asked.

"He's been quiet all day. Not like him." Another stretched truth. "But he's better now. So I don't think you need to look at him." Anything to save a buck.

"Are you going to give me something for my dog, or what?" said Aunt Josephine. Both ladies nodded to each other. They were in agreement.

"Let me check her over in the back," I said. "You can wait here; it's not as hot as in the exam rooms."

Fidget did have a problem. That fact would make Auntie deliriously happy. She had a painful neck. June showed me the urine test strip. Perfectly normal. Ah, the dilemma. How to treat one organ system while pretending to treat another? It reminded me of treating a cow for an udder infection many years before.

The ladies were bonding quite nicely when I returned Fidget.

"You are right," I said. "Fidget is not well."

"What did I tell you?" the bonded ladies said in unison.

"Give her these," I said, carefully not identifying the medication. Vitamin B12, I think I gave her, a placebo, quite harmless. Auntie would interpret the small red coated pills as medicine for Fidget's bladder. I knew no amount of persuasion would convince her that she didn't have a bladder infection. "And these for her pain." I handed her a potent anti-inflammatory painkiller for Fidget's sore neck.

"I knew she was in pain." She turned to her new friend. "What did I say?" The two ladies gave a unified nod.

The ladies left together chuckling over some private

joke, pets firmly in their arms, check books firmly in their purses.

June and I looked at each other and made our way quietly to the fridge in the back room. It was late afternoon and we kept a generous stock of light beer there—for medicinal purposes, you understand.

We ignored the fact that it looked like pee.

31

Quid pro Quo

No belief is right or wrong. It is either empowering or limiting. ~
Santosh Sachdeva

"This medicine is worthless!" Aunt Josephine announced to the waiting room at large. Unfortunately, having chosen that moment to deliver the records of my previous client to the front desk, I was at her mercy.

Holding aloft a brown plastic pill vial, she stared at it before delivering the rest of her accusation directly to me. "In cases such as this, it is the doctor who is responsible."

Before I could gather my wits, scattered by her direct assault, she added another salvo. "So what are you going to do about it?"

"May I see," I whispered, rather too loudly, holding out my hand for the offending medicine, and provoking Auntie's little dog, the victim of my *bad medicine*, into a paroxysm of yapping. Auntie gave her an understanding look.

I inhaled to capacity–a highly practiced defensive maneuver to prevent a stupid comment bubbling past my lips as an automatic response while waiting for logic to catch up to emotion.

"Humph," she puffed.

Auntie handed over the pill vial. While I tried to decipher the faded script on the empty vial she added, "I do not believe vitamin B12 can cure a bladder infection."

The incident with the alleged bladder infection had

happened some weeks before when she and Mrs. Ziglepush had first met in my office. They had wrongly identified her little dog's complaint with a unified display of diagnostic acumen, backed by years of being utterly sure of themselves. Since they would remain unconvinced of any alternative diagnosis I had prescribed an innocent placebo while treating Fidget's real problem, neck pain.

Clients respond better to medicine, even useless ones, than they do to mere advice, no matter how much expertise a clinician possesses. Despite her proclaimed sensitivity to the ills of human behavior, and her custom of dispensing her own counsel at the drop of a hat, Aunt Josephine also fell victim to the need to see that something, anything rather than nothing, was done. Hence I dispensed a placebo, a harmless drug, a stratagem called, oddly enough, treating the patient's expectations.

The placebo effect has been shown to work in about 30% of human cases. I never cease to be amazed that it also works with veterinary patients. Maybe owners exercise more mental control over their companions than we know, or the pets recover on their own anyway, or as in the instance of Aunt Josephine's little dog, it never had the condition in the first place.

"So," I said confidently, "I see she's better." Fidget twisted her head and neck to glare at me, obviously without pain.

"No thanks to you."

"So she is better!"

"Humph."

Fidget yapped.

There was a time when I thought I could make a small fortune providing placebo drugs to a 'gentleman' who wanted to alter the outcome of greyhound races. He had approached me less than seven days after I earned my license and offered a regular weekly remittance, far in excess of my monthly salary, to provide a few suitable narcotic pills. I could lose my license for supplying drugs, but I could argue that if I supplied placebos, I would in fact prevent a felony. Luckily, lucidity overcame stupidity. I decided that the ruse of the placebo, when discovered, could lead to several broken limbs, or even my rapid demise—which said gentleman, being professional in the art of drugging animals, among several other villainous activities, was sure to take care of—and my demise would be such a waste of an education.

"See," she said. "Fidget still doesn't like you." Fidget yapped at me. No one else. Me. Perhaps I should be grateful that she wasn't larger or didn't have a deafening bark.

What Fidget's misplaced yapping habit had to do with Auntie's questions about her treatment was beyond me.

At that moment one of our special clients arrived—perhaps eccentric would be a better description. Her eccentricity took the form of always appearing dressed for maximum exposure on the beach, or an obvious seduction. She was, however, conscientious about her pets. She leaned on the barrier behind which the receptionists usually hide, right next to Auntie, with enough energy to overcome the limits of her upper garment. Its generous contents spilled onto the surface of the counter. Smiling broadly, apparently empowered by the exposure, she wiggled back in while trying to write a check. You understand why I do not use her name.

The problem of how to explain my medical hocus-pocus to Aunt Josephine, whose attention had been so distracted as to render her speechless, still remained. Fortunately, Auntie had not enlisted her new friend and confidante, Mrs. Ziglepush, to accompany her and lend moral support, so I could discuss this without the inevitable unified humphs and rolling eyes.

Auntie and I had both had our tongues seized by the *special client*. I recovered mine first, although by that time the source of our confusion had left.

"You now have a healthy pet, Auntie," I said. I had been holding my breath, doing my best to keep eyes front. I used the breath-holding as an excuse for being flushed.

"Who was that?"

"A client," I gasped.

"You don't do house calls, do you!" It was not a question.

"Only for family." I was backsliding here, but I wanted to keep her distracted.

"Humph. What are you going to give Fidget?"

"Why? She's all better now. You did a great job. She doesn't need anything more."

The conflicts raged behind her hooded eyes; should she congratulate herself on a job well done, complain about Fidget, counsel me, argue about vitamin B12 or ask about my visitor?

Fortunately, since our client had had her back to the waiting room, no one else had seen the dramatic presentation.

"I'll drop in on the way home, Auntie," I said. While she pondered the alternatives, I ushered my confused relative, and her yapping pet, to the door.

From that day on, the reason for all clinic visits by the nameless one, no matter what they were really for, was written on the office-call list as check-writing.

Dealing with Auntie can be a hit or miss affair, rather like sexing baby geese—one sex honks, or hisses, or maybe it's the other way round—but however much I might like to leave the challenge of dealing with her to others more experienced in such matters, I was stuck with it. However, I will admit to feeling that I had won a victory of sorts. After all, she had been rendered speechless by someone writing a check.

32

Hidden Memories

Memory is the diary that we all carry about with us. ~ *Oscar Wilde*

Aunt Josephine is firmly of the opinion that all professional people are initially trained to a uniform standard of mediocrity and it falls to her to correct their lack of education. She has, over the years, endeavored to raise the social tonal scale of those she has met with unrequested, but in her mind necessary, sage advice. And if that is badly received, she is always prepared to take one on a guided guilt trip. She has an uncanny knack of finding and targeting blame and self-reproach. And of course, many of the memories that might cause *her* small pangs of—remorse, shall we say—have been conveniently forgotten.

I must admit my career has not been an uninterrupted series of humorous encounters, even though I write more about them because they are easier to remember and I think they are more fun to talk about. There are also nasty ghosts buried deep, ghosts that I prefer to forget, or that are merely hidden.

I believe there are two ways one deals with memories of things one doesn't want to face. Some, like spam email, the mind sends into quarantine, buried and inaccessible. In other cases part of our mind becomes hyper acute to the situation, and in whatever we do, it is unconsciously probing ahead, scouting for danger. In either case there are always triggers that will raise these memories to the surface, to the here and now, often as vividly as the day they happened.

Aunt Josephine is always prepared to pull a trigger.

Although a courtesy call on Auntie was tantamount to visiting a firing range, I had honored her request to visit because she had expressed a desire to take me visiting. Her neighbor, she assured me, was a dog lover—warning bell number one—who was eager to meet me—warning bell number two—and was an outspoken advocate for animal rights—warning bell number three.

The neighbor's house hid in a stand of trees at the end of a long driveway lined by large fenced cages housing dogs of varied size, breed and shape. We alighted from Auntie's car assaulted by a hysterical chorus of barking canines, and advanced on the house. Fortunately the offensive was made on our ears.

The door was opened by a woman whose youth startled me. I thought a friend of Auntie's would be closer to her age, than mine. She wore a soiled apron over her jeans and loose fitting blouse, and carried a dog bowl in her free hand. The other held the door. From her expression, you know, the eyebrow bit, a fleeting scowl replaced by a broad smile, and the obligatory backward step indicating surprise, I believed she did not expect such a visit.

As I smiled back, a cup-sized Yorkshire terrier dashed into view screaming invective at us for trespassing on his territory. I knew this display of fierce territorial rights was all noise, but I responded with a quick defensive move to handle the situation. I froze on the spot. This was not missed on Auntie. The reflex was the result of a memorable happening many years before.

At the time I saw practice with Alan Saunders back in the sixties, house calls were still a normal part of practice. On one such home visit, we were met at the door by a motherly lady with a broad grin. "Come to see the dog, have you? He's right through here." She indicated a door which appeared to lead to the back yard. She opened it for us and ushered us through. "He's been throwing up for a few days and his bowels are loose. Oh yes, and he's lethargic—no energy at all."

Without hesitation we stepped through the door into a small walled enclosure, about ten feet by twelve, with a back gate. We might as well have stepped into a cell. The small space served as storage for garbage cans and the coal bunker. In the corner, a skeletal German shepherd lay on top a large packing crate. Several patches of loose excrement and other odious matter dotted the ground. He lifted his head abruptly and appraised us with rheumy yellow eyes, then obviously annoyed at our rude intrusion and putting aside his reputed lethargy, he leaped from his crate with a roaring growl determined to tear us limb from limb. I have had more pleasant welcomes. A chain anchored to a metal eye-bolt in the brick wall arrested his sudden charge a scant foot from where we had, with alacrity, flattened ourselves against the door through which we had been ushered. It was firmly closed behind us, sealing our cell. When Alan reached behind himself and turned the handle the door remained firmly closed. Our motherly client had locked it. Then we heard a bolt being shot home.

We turned our attention to the dog slavering for our flesh. The chain was pulled tight. The eye-bolt appeared to be loose. We divided our attention between the dog and the bolt. A bookmaker would have been hard pressed to make either a favorite. In a remarkably controlled voice Alan Saunders asked if she would please open the door.

"Not scared of him are you?" she replied.

Not deigning to reply Alan repeated his request.

The owner answered with a shrill cackle.

The dog continued to work its jaws barely out of reach of our legs. His barking, by now hysterical with frustration at not being able to reach us, was deafening in that confined space.

After what felt like an hour or two we heard the bolt draw back, the lock click and the door opened. We had been perilously close to having to change our underwear.

Still deliberately controlled, Alan Saunders said, quite

reasonably, under the circumstances, "Bring him down to the office. He will be easier to examine out of his own yard. Where he doesn't have to defend his own territory you see."

"Me?" she said. "Bring him to you?"

"I think it would be best." On her broomstick perhaps.

"Now how do you think I could do that? I can't get near him."

"Can your husband do it?"

"Last time he touched the dog was when he put him on the chain."

"When was that?"

"About a year ago I think. Yes, must have been about a year."

"How on earth do you clean this place?"

"He doesn't mind us when we feed him. But since we gave him a bone last week he's not been well. He's been throwing up and he won't eat you see."

We faced a dilemma. The history of vomiting, diarrhea and lethargy after feeding a bone suggested he might have a bowel obstruction. The dog needed an examination and treatment, which would have been difficult, even in the office. But even if restored to health, this dog would have little quality of life.

The neglect and squalor it suffered on a daily basis was such that Alan reluctantly informed the local dog warden. Neglect and cruelty cases always leave a sour taste.

Auntie had of course reacted to my freezing at the sight of an aggressive Yorkie, recognizing it as a trigger. Her urge to bestow on me some deep and lasting wisdom was palpable, but as I stared at the little dog I heard her gasp. With a wild sweeping motion she swept it off the floor, hiding it by pressing it into the folds and mounds that separated her neck from where her waist should have been.

The eyes of our hostess opened wide in astonishment.

"You thought I was going to stomp on him didn't you?" I tried to look horrified as I spoke.

Our new hostess gasped.

"Of course I..." Speechless, Auntie's mouth opened and shut like a dying carp.

"Yes?" I asked.

"I didn't want him to nip your ankles."

Good recovery. I couldn't push her too far as I still had remote hopes of figuring in her will. Now the drawstring of annoyance, like a purse-string, pulled her fish-gasping lips together into a small crinkled bud.

The door closed in our faces. I felt sure I heard a bolt being shot home. The visit had ended before it began. We retreated through the din of the canine gauntlet to the car.

I forestalled a possible lecture by volunteering the details of the earlier situation down to the last gory detail. The severity of the encounter obviously made an impression on her. The shriveled bud of her lips relaxed. Her lips, now a thin line, appeared merely to be stitched together.

I knew she was wondering how a minute Yorkie possibly compared to the memory of a chained German shepherd—even if the piranha-like cup-cake was about to savage my legs. But of course her silence may have been due to her frustration at having a clear shot deflected, even before she had cocked and aimed when she thought I was about to attack the little dog. She didn't realize that it was quite impossible for me to have done anything, particularly tread on him. I was frozen to the spot.

33

Squashed

Someday we'll look back on this moment and plow into a parked car.
~ Evan Davis

Reflecting the opinion of some of the clients I have met, Aunt Josephine considers that much of the knowledge I have learned is fit only for Jeopardy or cross-word puzzles, neither of which am I good at. It probably is really, although I am indebted to all those people who have bolstered my education with trivia because I hope that one day this information might help me write tall tales. The role of aspiring writer had taken the place of my theatrical roles as I matured, and the parts I was offered became fewer.

Jenny, Anne's sister had once asked me about whether I had any experiences with wild animals other than zoo animals. I hadn't really, except to anesthetize a few exotic patients. These had included snakes, birds, a tiger, kangaroos and an elephant, which, although they had contributed to my store of arcane knowledge, were not everyday practice cases. Apart from the brief interaction I had with a keeper at the reptile house in the London Zoo when I was a student, I couldn't share any stories about the people around them either, which is where the real interest lies.

But I did remember one of my childhood educators who had some experience with animals in the wild. Mr. Pettigrew was a small dapper Frenchman, a friend of my parents in Tanzania, who always dressed in a white suit and could have been Agatha Christie's model for Poirot. I told Jenny about him because I had been reminded of this story when Helen and I were driving back from a wedding and were rear-ended on Interstate 84, so the memory was still fresh in my mind.

If you hit an elephant hard enough behind the knees it will sit down, Mr. Pettigrew had told me—and if you hit it behind the knees with a car, it will sit on the hood. He added that it might leave a message that Mr. van der Merwe would have delighted in. *C'est la vie!* He knew because he said he once came around a curve too fast to stop and went straight into the hind end of a Jumbo.

When he said it squashed his hood, I had believed him, I mean why not? I was a kid. Other people laughed. He was known to see things they said, particularly after the cocktail hour which started when the sun went down. It was rumored that when the sun took its time to set he had been known to see pink elephants, and pink elephants couldn't hurt things they said. I didn't understand what they meant because I had never heard of a pink elephant and it was years before I saw one, but I ran right away to look at his car and it *was* squashed. A large greenish-brown patch on the hood proved Mr. Pettigrew's point. Not pink. Kind of dried up though, which would have disappointed Mr. van der Merwe. But the others didn't look. They laughed. Later, when they did see his car, they not only believed, they made him a kind of hero. And helped him celebrate sundown.

It's a pity Mr. Pettigrew didn't know Mr. van der Merwe. I think they would have bonded like Aunt Josephine and Mrs. Ziglepush.

On the occasion that we had found the elephant scat in the Itigi-Sumbu Thicket, while heading out for a picnic, we had continued down the narrow track between the high thorn scrub. The car wheels in the dirt ruts either side of a narrow strip of brown grass churned the dust into an ochre cloud that blotted out our passage. As the tall thorn scrub whipped past in a blur, the longer branches scraping the sides to make it feel like we were flying when we were only travelling 15 or 20 miles an hour, a full-grown bull Giraffe stepped out of the scrub in front of us.

My father braked hard. The station-wagon slid in the loose dust. As the car slowed, the Giraffe loped away in front of us.

"Let's chase him," we brave kids cried.

We closed up behind the giraffe and matched his speed. He responded to the chase by lengthening his stride. He began to draw away. We in the back seat demonstrated our bravery again by encouraging my father. We were flying! We began to catch him. We drew closer.

Then the giraffe stopped. He skidded to a halt, his hind legs tucked under him like a gangly cutting horse. He spun in his tracks and hurtled back down the track directly toward us.

Time dilated as Einstein said it would.

We were on a collision course. From the back seat all we could see were legs—slowly moving—growing bigger and closer. The four-ton animal bore down on us.

Our turn to skid in the dust. We slid towards him.

Then he stopped and spun around again. We slid gently into his left hind leg.

Like Mr. Pettigrew's elephant, the animal sat down. With thorn scrub on both sides and a bull giraffe on the hood, the inside of the car went suddenly quite dark.

No one moved. Not even the giraffe. He was probably as surprised as we were. Or Mr. Pettigrew's elephant.

His legs folded in a different way to an elephant's. His front legs and his right hind leg were still on the ground. His left leg stuck straight out from the hood, clear of the ground as he perched on the right fender.

Mr. van der Merwe reacted first. He loosed a shot into the air through the window. The car shook as the bull lurched to its feet, took two or three strides and turned off the track into a gap in the thorn scrub. A gap he must have seen as he passed it. All his legs worked.

It was quiet inside the car. We sat there for a little while. I thought about what had happened. I expect the others did too. If he hadn't spun in his tracks I don't think he would have jumped over the car. Those legs would have smashed though the roof and the windshield. And us.

With the giraffe gone, we emptied ourselves from the car and surveyed the damage. The hood could have passed for Mr. Pettigrew's. But luckily, at least, I thought luckily, there were no scatological messages left for us. There was a large crack in the right side of the windshield. The right headlight stuck out like an eye on a stalk, and the fender pressed on the wheel a bit. The radiator was intact. The air cleaner was squashed but the engine worked—and cars were expected to survive abuse in Africa. There was no question of going home. We were out for a picnic.

Eventually we left the dense thorn scrub behind and drove into more open grassland, which although it still shared the space with thorn and acacia, was a little less daunting. It gave us somewhere to set up our picnic site and start a fire—the first order of any stop, start a fire, heat water for tea, and prepare a good bed of glowing embers for cooking meat on a stick, and baking potatoes in the ashes.

We had the tea going, and started to eat, with still more meat and potatoes scorching in the fire when we heard the grunt. Mum thought it was the kettle. I hadn't a clue. You can hear strange noises in the bush. I noticed Mrs.van der Merwe calmly open the back of the station wagon and take out the guns. She stood them carefully against the side of the wagon.

Mr. van der Merwe walked away a few yards and put his head to the ground. Then he made a sort of explosive grunty noise, and a lion answered him. It was close, and although he said it had probably eaten and wouldn't bother us, particularly with the fire going, we kids felt more comfortable in the car—hiding under what cushions and blankets we could find.

It may have been the lion that had spooked the giraffe onto our trail, or even the smell of the elephant. I don't know to this day how fastidious giraffes are.

We told ourselves what a great picnic it had been. Couldn't wait to go on another. We never did.

As I re-played the events of that childhood picnic in my mind, I realized that Helen and I had not been to another wedding either since we had been rear-ended.

34

Without a Cry

It's so simple to be wise. Just think of something stupid to say and then don't say it. ~ Sam Levinson

    I have started mornings feeling better, thanks to the unexpected virus that left me congested, snuffling, and with eyes that would suddenly overflow. So perhaps I should have been paying more attention to the case in hand when my cursory glance at the front cover of the case notes was arrested by the bright yellow note stuck on the front. It carried one word Mute.
    The front desk staff, bless their collective hearts, after years of requests to warn me about peculiar clients, like Aunt Josephine and Mrs. Ziglepush, were now most efficient at alerting me to any situation out of the ordinary. It gave me a momentary pause to adjust my expectations of the impending office call.
    I wondered if this client was also deaf. One of the staff happened to be fluent in American Sign Language, an invaluable aid in such cases, but today had to be her day off. Had she been there, the case notes would have been in her hand, instead of carrying the yellow note. I was on my own. I scrambled to gather paper and pen, for easier communication, should my client have need to inform me of the salient features and problems of her pet. I did the exercises that I usually used before going on stage to loosen up the lips and face, to help enunciate clearly should my client be lip reading. They made my nose run. As I entered

the examination room I noted the staff eyeing me with some concern.

A man and a woman and a pretty white feline fluff-ball smiled at me, then the man greeted me. Hah, at least my brain is still working. I deduce that it is the woman who is mute. So carefully pronouncing all my nasally words, accenting them with exaggerated lip movements and making sure I faced her at all times, I asked some summary questions. Everyone, including the kitty, listened patiently.

"She first lost her voice after she started sneezing," the woman said. I looked at her sharply, and despite years of training I could feel the heat growing as the reflex flush of pure embarrassment suffused my cheeks. (I like that word, suffused, I have never had the opportunity to use it before) Anyway my suffusion did a beetroot proud. And I empathized with the poor silent kitty with viral laryngitis.

I stammered my way through the rest of the examination then, taking the bull by the proverbial horns, I explained my dilemma and showed them the yellow note. They thought it the funniest thing, and it explained so much, especially they said, my incredible lip movements, of which I should be proud. The kitty joined in, mouthing silent laughter.

Animals, like humans, can lose their voice to infection, to injury, or as in the case of my aunt's dog which usually had a bout of hysterical yapping when it saw me, because they are not feeling well. Veterinarians rarely become speechless but owners have been known to be struck dumb, usually when seeing a bill. And sometimes the history of the pet's condition is too closely woven with their own for them to say anything about it.

I had taken the case notes up to the front desk, followed by my 'talkative' clients and their meadow-less kitty, where I nearly sneezed over the Reverend.

"My, my, and isn't it the bundle of lethargy you're looking this morning," he said.

"Oh hello, Reverend."

My spiritual friend's good spirits and enthusiasm for life bubbled through any conversation even as his body looked as if the contents had settled during shipping. In contrast, my head and sinuses felt as is they had settled too. He was exchanging courtesies and dispensing blarney in equal amounts to June, my receptionist. Standing next to him, trying his hardest to be invisible, a red faced teenager squirmed at the sound of the Reverend's voice. This of course caught the Reverend's twinkling eye

"If it isn't Michael himself. How are you lad? Nothing too drastic that brings you here I hope."

Michael mumbled something about needing to get home. He disappeared in a metaphorical flash and the Reverend transferred his gaze back to me. His eyebrows arched upwards; shaggy question marks above his twinkling eyes.

I smiled back. We don't discuss cases with others except professional colleagues, but I was in need of counsel myself. Maybe I could broach the subject in a roundabout, tangential, circumspect sort of way.

I had examined Michael's dog prior to mouthing at the kitty's owners. The young man had been house-sitting while his parents were away. He had found his dog that morning staggering, depressed, and disoriented. In the examination room the dog had waited patiently next to the examination table, head down, fore-feet slightly splayed, swaying gently. When he tried to walk he staggered as if drunk. The reflexes from the major nerves were intact and apparently normal. His pupils were dilated. The acute onset suggested poisoning of some type. Unfortunately many drugs, pot, sedatives or even alcohol can cause such signs. Opiates normally constrict the pupil.

"Has he been exposed to anything strange?" I had asked.

"No."

"Could he have gotten into the garbage?"

"No."

"Taken him anywhere different?"

"No."

"Fed him anything different?" For the first time he hesitated.

"I had a few friends over to stay last night. Maybe they gave him something."

Now we were getting somewhere. But beyond that he was not prepared to go.

I reviewed the notes I had made, speculated and reached a conclusion. One of the technicians, Nicky or Claudia, I forget who, gave the dog something to try to make him vomit and had an I.V. running. When he didn't vomit after a couple of doses of emetic I left the young ladies muttering under their breath, struggling to dose the dog with a messy black slurry of activated charcoal to adsorb the presumed toxin .

The clinical exam had yielded little more than the observations in the exam room.

I won't bore you with the deliberations but my unanimous opinion—best guess—the dog appeared to have eaten pot. That was my technician's considered opinion really—I know nothing of these things, particularly if Aunt Josephine is within earshot. Question; was it the boy's stash, or that of a friend? Had someone given it to him, or had he found it for himself? If it was pot, the dog would recover easily enough. If it was alcohol, or another drug, I didn't know if his condition was worsening, stable, or he was already recovering. Michael was not forthcoming on the subject, which is usually the case with recreational drug users, particularly teenagers who don't want their parents to know.

Naturally Michael would not admit to having any pot in the house. He was obviously worried but the more we questioned, the more he fell back on "I found the dog like this."

Scaring him hadn't worked either.

"You understand, that in severe nerve cases like this,

where there is a sudden onset, we are faced with a problem. Is it something that humans can catch? In which case we have to tell the police, the National Guard, warn the mayor so he can quarantine the town, close schools, possibly use the emergency evacuation plans. It is all quite serious." Actually there was no legal requirement that I notify the police, so I crossed my fingers behind my back. The question of talking to his parents might be a different matter.

He had squirmed a bit but didn't budge from his story. He must view his parents with a sense of personal terror.

"To take the diagnosis further we must X-Ray the dog, take blood work, start him on intravenous fluids and consider a toxicology screen. We have to call your parents for permission with an estimate. Or you can authorize it and pay for the work."

He would pay.

To be on the safe side—cover our delicate rear ends—we took the blood, or rather Claudia or Nicky did. We held it in the fridge and passed on the x Rays.

"What brings you here father?" I croaked, much like the laryngitic kitty.

"Oh a simple thing, here don't I have it on the list that sister Agnes gave me. But the young lady here is doing me proud so she is."

June looked at me, "Fleas, ticks and heartworm stuff," she read aloud. "And Michael left a deposit."

"The lad's dog now, it's here?" asked my spiritual friend. I nodded. "That reminds me, do you have a few minutes?" he said. "Don't I have a curious question to ask." It saved me making a direct approach to him. I invited him in the office. He settled into a chair, sucking on a cold pipe.

"How can I help you?" I croaked.

"Forgive an old busybody—it's a manner I've grown into. But recently it's got me to wondering if drugs affect animals as surely as they do humans?"

A curious question—coincidence perhaps? "Recreational drugs, you mean."

"A terrible name for them, but yes."

I explained briefly what they did and how pets usually found them, then in a flash of brilliance asked what had got him to wondering about them?

"I do a lot of counseling, particularly for the boys now. And the lad, smelling as he did, it was that you see." He began to knock out the cold ashes of his pipe in the wastebasket.

"Smelling?"

He looked up. "You didn't smell it then?"

"I'm not up to much smelling today," I sniffed.

"Ah yes." He paused a moment. "I don't think I'm breaking any confidences now, you see, when I tell you his clothes reeked of the pot, so they did."

Confirmation of my diagnosis from an unlikely source—sort of. I could see he was itching to ask about the dog, but he respected what might be a professional confidence. When I didn't volunteer that it *wasn't* pot affecting Michaels dog he chuckled and shook his head as he read between the lines.

We kept the patient overnight. His recovery was swift and unremarkable. I wasn't able to discuss Michael's own experience with him, but mentioned the suspicion that maybe he had a friend with a bad habit who had played a joke on his dog to see what happened. That way everyone saved face and it left the task of a family discussion to his parents. They knew what had happened right away. At first they were annoyed, but they soon mellowed and chuckled over it, after all not only had their son lost his stash but he had to foot the bill. They felt that he had learned a positive lesson.

I had little else to add to their conclusions, so I sniffed, and remained mute.

35

Unintended Consequences

L'enfer est plein de bonnes volontés ou désirs. (Hell is full of good intentions or desires.) ~ St. Bernard of Clairvaux

We normally shut up shop on Saturday afternoons, but on this particular damp and forlorn day, one that dragged down the spirits with an incessant drizzle, we had stayed open to hold a low-cost vaccination clinic. We did that on occasion. We hoped it would be seen as a service and a way of helping to widen the net of protected animals. A few clients, including Aunt Josephine, thought it was a cheap way for us to make a quick buck. And some of our patients, less able to express themselves in human terms, considered it an exercise in sadism, and told us so with quite fierce doggy talk and the various scented messages they left about the room when scared.

While waiting, some pets, like their owners, sat motionless appearing to read the advertising material, contributing to the miasma of wet dog, clinging like the dreary mist to everything in the room. Others hid under the chairs, deciding if they would agree to see the vet. A Rottweiler lay in the corner like a suburban battle tank at rest. Across the room, a Teutonic German shepherd stood heels together, ears at attention. There were a surprising number of people grouped around the animals.

I checked on how the registration was going then went to hide in my office where I found the Reverend lay in wait.

"It is meself that is convinced," my Reverend friend

said, "that humans dreadfully outnumber all the domestic species combined, so they do." He had wedged himself in a chair on the other side of my desk, sipping from a Far Side mug. It showed a classical Gary Larson scene, "The Boneless Chicken Ranch" with floppy chickens strewn every which way in the ranch yard.

"What brought that on?" I ventured to ask. There were no humans near the chickens.

"Now, let me see, isn't it the number of family members congregated around those poor sick beasts in your waiting room, so it is."

"There are no sick ones this afternoon," I said. "They are all healthy, waiting for a vaccination clinic, that starts," I looked at my watch, "in about ten minutes."

"Well, I never. Isn't it more like a wake out there. Why, some are even shedding tears so they are. I felt moved to bless them on their way to the hereafter."

"Isn't it a devilish sense of humor you have there, Reverend."

"Devilish. Devilish. Another adjective would possibly be more suited, don't you think." His eyes twinkled.

"We were taught that we had to deal with six point four humans to every animal," I said. "That starts with an average of two and a half family members, receptionists, technicians, nurses, kennel staff—you see the picture?"

"I might wish that members of my former congregation would have had such concerned family members guiding them to the pews, so I do." He stared down into his mug as if he could read the future in the tea leaves—except that he was drinking coffee.

"I think it took a famous businessman to notice that there is a dignity, even in animals, which some human beings might study to advantage," he added.

Auntie walked in to catch the end of the conversation, Fidget firmly under her arm. I had invited the Reverend back when he dropped in to return the large plastic cone that Jessie had worn for a few days after her surgery, to prevent her chewing out her stitches. Of course, since his retirement had allowed his memory to relax, he had forgotten what day it was. Auntie assumed that being a relative assured her of a certain rank in the practice—she marched in cloaked in a tent-like garment to thwart the rain.

"Sister Agnes is not with you today, Father?" I asked.

"Isn't it herself is busy at the shelter, so she is. Three days a week, and Saturday. Oh my, now isn't that today?"

"Poor homeless creatures," Auntie said.

"Ah, the sin of poverty buries them deeply, so it does."

"Sin?"

"How else can one account for the vagaries of behavior that blight them so?

"Your efforts to dig them out, and those of Sister Agnes, are most commendable," Auntie said. Even giving praise she managed to sound indignant.

"Me do the digging? Oh, I am not that handy with a shovel."

"But you are obviously trying," she persisted.

"Oh, I don't see it as my job to dig so strenuously. It's like teaching; if the sinner doesn't handle most of the digging himself, all the teacher's efforts are in vain."

"How on earth can you expect those poor creatures to help themselves? Anyway, I do not believe that animals are subject to sin. It is merely behavior."

"A delightful belief, delightful. But it was the human animal I was talking about.

"But you said a shelter."

"One for the homeless, yes."

"Oh, you are impossible."

The Reverend was learning that sometimes, communication with Aunt Josephine could be as frustrating as playing bingo with a stammer.

Claudia put her head round the door. "In back," she said. "Quickly."

A large dog of indeterminate breed lay collapsed on a sheet soiled with blood. It wore a large plastic cone on its head, like the one my Reverend friend had returned, to prevent it chewing at a surgical site on its belly. The effort appeared to have been futile. Most of its intestines lay on the sheet beside it protruding from a small hole in the center of a line of stitches running along the middle of its abdomen. The surgical repair of an abdominal wound had broken down, bringing the victim perilously close to death.

Claudia and Nicky were already at work placing an intravenous catheter and setting up fluids. There was no time to ask—do it!

I gave the patient a quick examination although I had already decided on a course of action—treat for shock, induce anesthesia, explore the damage, clean and repair—I still had time to wonder how such a small opening in the middle of the original surgery site could penetrate right through to the abdomen. The question was soon answered. As one of the techs took off the plastic cone before anesthesia I noticed the edge had been chewed. It was as serrated and sharp as a circular saw. It had caught on a stitch or two, pressed right through the wound, and ripped the stitches away on its way out. An unintended consequence of trying to stop him chewing his stitches out in the first place.

The Reverend examined the damaged collar. The saw-like edge was different from the one he had returned. He didn't need to say anything. His expression said it all. We stared at each other for a few moments exchanging silent thoughts through body language. Then he patted my shoulder. I was aware he had not given me a blessing.

The patient took this second surgery in stride, so perhaps I had been given a silent blessing. No trace of post-op infection developed.. To avoid this patient repeating his own stitch removal, I used thin stainless steel stitches in the skin. Their sharp points should deter him from chewing at the new repair, unless he was modern enough to want his tongue pierced.

This was not the first time, and it would not be the last,

that a procedure to achieve something had the opposite result, or led to other problems.

By the end of the emergency surgery, some vaccination clients had left. Those remaining, by and large, understood the delay and took it in stride. Word of the cause had spread. There were a few who would never again look at a plastic cone—a so-called Elizabethan collar—without suspicion. It is so easy to induce paranoia.

Aunt Josephine and the Reverend had stayed during the emergency surgery despite their confused conversation. I thought it was out of concern, but it may have been to witness the ensuing chaos of the delayed vaccination clinic. They were not disappointed.

When June announced we were ready there was a surge of bodies, a mixture of clients and pets. An exuberant Labrador, waiting for the moment, leaped to his feet, and rushed round the room leaving his coat strewn across the floor in his haste. He grabbed the nearest magazine in his slobbery mouth and trotted from client to client as if offering them a gift. One or two clients, slow to join the impending melee, looked up from their seats. Some ignored him. Others hugged their pets closer. The lap pets appeared to be relieved that a magazine was all he picked up. He rushed over to the receptionist's counter, put his front paws on top and delivered his slobbery burden to June.

"Come." He responded to the call from a tiny woman, the nails on his back feet screeching on the tiled floor as he scrambled towards the exam room, eager to be the first vaccination victim, the first of the afternoon.

Auntie took a brief look in the waiting room.

"On second thoughts, Fidget can wait a while," she said. "Anyway they are not really due."

I attributed her decision to her belief in the catastrophic nature of surgery in general, although it might have been the urge to save a buck. I had expected a verbal assault from her, but I think the situation had been serious enough that she was scared of what she might say, so she looked at me with a pinched face and remained silent on that subject.

I hurried after the energetic Labrador.

I cannot for the life of me tell you why I didn't tell my guests that the emergency surgical patient had never been my patient. He had never even been to our clinic. Maybe they would think I was making excuses. Paranoia is so easy to induce.

36

Manic Monday

Your idea of bliss is to wake upon a Monday morning knowing that you haven't a single engagement for the entire week. ~ Edna Ferber

I expect you've had days like this too. A day where trial piles on tribulation, worry on concern, and you run out of coffee. There is no doubt in my mind that it is all due to that demagogue of doom, Mr. Murphy. There is a vile veterinary version of his law—the number of urgent cases will increase in inverse proportion to the availability of staff.

"Start in room one," June said. "Bleeding dog."

"It's the local cat. It's wild and real mean," the owner volunteered as I was scarcely through the examination room door. I had yet to ask a question. Cat?

I looked at my patient. A black Border collie lay panting on the table, a crude bloodied bandage around its body.

"Can we start again," I asked, trying to be gentle. The dog was hurt, the owner distressed, and I was puzzled. He was a regular and conscientious client. I couldn't figure the cat angle.

"The cat chased him. He didn't want to hurt it so he tried to jump the fence. He didn't quite make it."

Spooked by the cat. This was obviously no ordinary cat. What sort of cat I wondered? Perhaps like Alan Saunder's remarkable Siamese who put the cows in their place so many years before.

I had June secure a soft muzzle on the dog's nose

before removing the bandage. I had to see the damage, and a dog in pain does not always discriminate between merely trying to tell you it hurts, and grasping your hand roughly with its teeth. A five inch long gash was witness to a misjudged jump.

Now came my staff juggling act. I tallied the forces. One tech had insisted that she needed to leave to have her baby. I agreed with her, because short staffed as we were, a human whelping—giving birth—would have interrupted the schedule. Another had snuck a day off. I lie; it was a scheduled absence, with permission. That left one receptionist and two techs where normally there would have been 5 or 6 people if you count me. As it takes two usually to restrain and treat wounds such as I have described, this meant a bit of fancy footwork on the part of all as we slotted these cases between regular calls, vaccinations and puppy examinations, which had decided to come in at the last minute. We had four exam rooms, one of which had a door to the outside to admit infectious patients. This also served to isolate aggressive animals, those who could threaten life, limb and liability if they strutted their stuff in the waiting room. The staff filled the others as quickly as possible so that even if clients complained about the bill, they couldn't complain that they were kept waiting to receive it. Clever don't you think?

I sedated the patient with a narcotic premed to ease its pain until we could sneak back between cases. Once anesthetized, the repair was fairly straightforward. This was a high point—the client was really grateful. I was almost done when the cat came in. Not the cause of the excitement with this collie, but one, as the Reverend would say, "isn't it altogether another one entirely."

A large battered tomcat, as heavy-jowled as a life-long politician, glared at me. Its ears, face, chin and neck had been self-shredded by its back claws to relieve an itch of unknown and unfathomable cause. Its face glowed with hairless, scabby inflamed areas. I doubted that there would be an opportunity to find the cause. Treat what could be seen, that was the plan, and I instructed my reduced staff, if they found any Tibetan prayer-wheels in the clinic, to spin them in passing.

Restraining an itchy cat, particularly a large, partly feral tomcat is—interesting. Even well-bred cats do not always know that only at home can one scratch where one truly itches. Our patients do not stop using their back claws to relieve a problem merely because we tell them to. By restraining the poor moggy we merely succeeded in deflecting its aim from its head. Most of us who work in the field carry marks of honor on our arms to attest to such encounters.

Could the cause be ear-mites? These are little critters that live and thrive in an environment of ear wax—not a lifestyle I would choose—but the ears were clean, no tell-tale signs of the hallmark black crud. The most probable cause was an allergy, possibly to food.

Clip and clean. An injection to relieve the itching, and a suitable easily administered antibiotic.

Next!

A litter of pups were waiting in wide-eyed wonder for health examinations and their first vaccinations. I began to examine them, all smiles of course, because young pups, starting their adventure with life, are a lot of fun. We played scratch-belly, chew the Doc's stethoscope, and tug-a-tail with each other, until a dog with a three day old infected bite wound came in. Reluctantly, I spent the next few minutes stuffing puppies back in their box—I swear many more than originally came in—before leaving.

The infected wound was not really a big deal as cases go but the owner would not allow it to be taken in back to the prep area to be clipped and cleaned because he had had bad experiences with vets. Exactly what, he declined to specify. We ferried the required materials into the exam room, much the same things as we used for the feral tomcat. The client maintained a non-stop interrogation of what I meant to do, what I would do it with, what was in the surgical solution I intended to use to clean up the traumatized site, and of course why he would have to pay so much. It was a hostile cross-examination. I continued to smile but it was an effort to keep my lip pinned up to that bare patch between lip and nose. His questions mixed with my instructions to the tech staff were creating some confusion, not least with me. I was still trying to keep up with the interrogation when I was told a dog in the next room, another walk-in, was bleeding profusely from its leg.

In this case the owner's son had decided to remove a skin tag with a pair of scissors. Not a good idea. To control the small spurting blood vessel he had then bandaged the leg, hoping, I surmised, to prevent his parents finding out that he was not the sharpest knife in the drawer. He had cranked the bandage tight enough to make the foot swell. That brought his parents into the picture. No one was happy. Of course, I treated it brilliantly with a little local anesthetic and cautery. Luckily their ire focused on the son, so our patient, staff and I were spared of blame.

As I fled from the exam area to claw the sticky remains from the coffee pot, I heard my client of the bad veterinary experience still muttering meaningful questions—then Sampson arrived.

Sampson was a voluble regular. A Beagle pup, so bright and cheerful, his enthusiasm for life bubbled over like the head on a hastily poured mug of ale. Most times he would greet us with a proud display of his hunting cry. Not today.

"Since yesterday he's been drooling and walks with his head down," his owner, Jake Evans, offered.

If ever there was an example of a hang-dog expression, he showed it; browbeaten, defeated or abject, the poor animal stood head bowed, face and front legs stained with overflowing saliva, not his usual frothy gusto.

"We were out hunting yesterday. He started out fine, but I thought he couldn't take the work. He's had better days running off at the mouth."

In the countryside of upstate New York, this was a typical manic Monday call; one of those cases where animals run into trouble from sharing the weekend activities too closely with their owners. Usually they overeat—euphemistically, commit a dietary indiscretion—from eating too many treats at the barbecue or gorging on garbage—delicious. Some get bones lodged across the roof of their mouth between their back teeth. Others suffer penetrating wounds, usually foreign bodies in the pads, thorns, or in the case of city dogs, small shards of glass.

Jake and I lifted the dog onto the examination table. Taking the temperature is a good place to start. Sampson had a fever. He winced and moved his head away when I felt around his neck and throat. Gently opening his mouth I could see that his tongue was swollen and bruised. A hole, perhaps an inch across, gaped on the side of it. Behind the hole, and stretching back towards his throat, the tongue was rigid and hard to the touch.

"Looks like he has a penetrating wound here." Sometimes I astound myself at how bright I am. "And judging by the swelling there might be something in it."

Sampson's injury reminded me of another penetrating wound which played a large part in steering me towards veterinary school. In a glass fronted case in my dining room at home, where the memorabilia of a lifetime are displayed, stand two silver plated beer mugs, a gift from a grateful friend to my father, more than half a century ago, in thanks for the nursing care he gave to a horse that suffered such an accident.

Most of my vacation activities as a teenager in the country of Malawi centered on horses. We had moved some distance outside the nearest town, built rough stables and cleared a large area in the scrub vegetation for an exercise arena and jumping course. It proved popular with other horse owners, some of whom traveled long distances to use the jumps.

Having scoured the cleared area for treacherous holes that could swallow an unwary hoof, we had marked the boundary with small colored flags, mounted on bamboo stakes driven into the ground. This was as safe a surface as we could prepare. Beyond the stakes, the ground was not free of obstacles.

Late one afternoon, a visiting horse, Fleet's Review, shied at a jump, ran wide, skirted the edge of the arena, knocked down a pole and trod on it with a front hoof. The other end of the stake lifted up and Fleet impaled herself on it.

A large wound gaped open in her groin between body and the hind leg, at least a foot deep, full of bamboo splinters. By incredible luck the pole had missed penetrating the abdomen, or hitting the femoral artery.

Fleet's Review was a five year old Thoroughbred mare, newly imported from South Africa, fresh off the race track, strong willed, flighty, and not easy to handle. With a week left before I had to return to school, my father assigned me the immediate nursing job of trying to keep the wound clean.

The next morning the leg had swollen from the groin to her hoof. Congealed serum and blood that had drained overnight matted the hair. It took twelve hours that day before the mare allowed me to work my way from a front leg to the injury. I coaxed her with carrots, petted her, talked to her, whatever I could think of to help her trust me. Something eventually worked. By seven that evening, I was able to syringe the wound with peroxide and clean out hundreds of small bamboo splinters. My father bandaged the leg from hoof to as high as she would allow. This would minimize swelling and catch the discharge, so it didn't stick to her leg and attract flies. We fought them with liberal quantities of *Dimethylphthalate*, a potent fly repellant. The name of the active ingredient is still burned in my brain. During the following days I would go through bottles of the stuff.

I spent the week caring for her before the new term beckoned. Twice a day I syringed the wound and changed her bandage. When I left, my father took over the nursing duties. By the time I came home at the end of the term three months later, the attention he had lavished on the mare had worked a remarkable change in her behavior. Fleet's Review no longer acted like a highly strung racehorse; she followed him about whenever she could, like a puppy.

I admitted the voiceless Beagle for surgical exploration. A foreign object had snapped off about two inches inside his tongue. He probably ran it into his mouth while running, head to the ground and howling. I shuddered at the thought of how it must have felt. I removed a stick over an inch thick and eight inches long. With the foreign object removed, the wound syringed with a suitable antiseptic and the hole left open to drain, he was dispatched home on an antibiotic.

Ten days treatment worked a remarkable change in the Beagle.

"Back in voice," Jake announced proudly at his recheck, while Sampson greeted all in the practice with a display of high strung yodeling to demonstrate his voice. He interrupted his singing to snuffle round the room—possibly looking for rabbits we might have overlooked, or perhaps to show how he had injured himself in the first place.

37

Troublesome Tuesday

Every case, no matter how simple, can lead you down a blind alley or two. ~ Thomas Magnum, Magnum P.I.

Two minutes after my arrival at the office, not even time to fill my coffee mug, and June, my receptionist, hovered like a bug with a case file in her hand. Being as sensitive as I am to routine, I sensed a change in my appointments. I sometimes amaze myself how sharp I can be (I think I told you that before)—even before my morning coffee. I view any adjustments to the schedule with suspicion—it is part of my defensive paranoia. My misgivings were not diminished when I saw she was wearing an enigmatic smile, which, like that of the Mona Lisa, could mean anything from seduction to up yours. I interpreted it to mean gotcha with this one.

"Your favorite case," she said. "He's been here half an hour. Came in with surgery drop-offs. Said he needed to see you before he went to work."

"Who is it?" I asked, taking the file from her. "A regular appointment?" The staff knew better than to book cases so early.

Like most practices, we admitted surgery cases during the hour before office calls started. This allowed the staff time to do tests and investigations and prep the cases for surgery. I opened the file.

"Oh." Client complaint, dog is scooting. My client had a dog that was dragging its behind on the ground. "Better get him in a room. I'll take care of it before the scheduled office calls begin."

It was indeed a regular client who had booked a recheck appointment, but, to speed up the process from his point of view, had decided to come in early. This case should have been straightforward and simple. There are only a few causes of butt dragging, and these had been most skillfully addressed, by me—and eliminated as causes—so I thought. His stool had been checked for intestinal worms—negative. I had checked the smelly scent marking glands which can become swollen and irritated if the ducts become blocked—normal. There was no evidence of fleas, and he had no signs of allergies, such as paw-licking, chewing his flanks and scratching his armpits.

This poor patient had nothing—as far as I could see—that would make him itch. However, this was his third visit and, as the case notes indicated, the problem persisted. I was at a complete loss as to what to do next—a state that must be most carefully hidden from my client. Clients, by and large, loathe indecision. It can be interpreted as not knowing what you are doing. Sometimes they are right.

"He has three dogs with him today. All with the same problem."

"What?" Contagious scooting! That was one for the books. Contagious Scootophilia, a contagious love of butt-dragging. *Scotophilia* is a medical term, from real medicine, that means love of darkness—I added another *o* to create an addition to all those long words we spent many years learning at school.

With all three dogs in the household doing it, I should have three times the evidence to diagnose the condition and conjure up a solution. But I doubted it.

I felt the miasma of an ominous mood settle over me and compete with the coffee—which I had not yet had.

When in doubt, go back to square one.

"Let's run over the history one more time, shall we? When did the dogs start to do this?"

"Oh, they didn't start together. Buster started first and the others copied him."

"Copied?"

"They always follow his lead. And they only do it on the lawn and in the yard, never in the house."

A pooch that could teach butt-dragging must be an alpha dog of the first order. Maybe he could be trained to teach other things. This suggested a whole new approach to dog training. Maybe he could have his own TV program. Synchronized Scooting.

If I cured the lead dog, would the others stop? It was worth a try. Problem was how to do it. I had already tried shots for itching to no effect.

The constant scooting had irritated Buster's behind, the bit he sat on, and as is the way with lesions, as they heal, they itch. Now Buster, and his two subordinate students, with similar areas of irritation, were all justified in scooting!

But if it was due to itching, how come they reserved their anti-social activity to the outside? It was a puzzlement.

Left with prescribing local treatment of the irritated butts and finger crossing, I recommended a spray that was usually useful in relieving itching. This I dispensed with the usual forced smile of encouragement, and stern advice to Buster to teach his buddies different tricks, which perhaps understandably, did not completely relieve my client's skepticism.

"So," he said. "You think this will work?"

He stared at the container in his hand and made no effort to leave. A bad sign. When a client's feet stick to the floor it shows we have a different opinion about whether the appointment is over. I placed my hand on his shoulder as an expression of confidence, and to nudge him towards the door. When neither worked I fell back on the old standby.

"I'll have someone show you how to use the spray before you leave," I said, and scurried out.

I think the staff was also skeptical because I saw a

couple muttering together and glancing at me while demonstrating the spray and examining the dogs' behinds for themselves. Checking up on me. It was duly noted. The staff knew this—they also knew how little effect 'being noted' ever had. But at least Nicky brought me a fresh cup of coffee.

Then Claudia came in. Late—not as usual—but late. By the exasperated expression of her face, pinched, tight lipped, eyebrows forming a series of waves across her forehead, I sensed intuitively that something was amiss. Behind her, at the end of a dangerously stretched leash, her well-fed spaniel, Mipsy, lumbered from leg to leg following Claudia's frustrated tugs. The dog's mouth bristled with porcupine quills.

"How did this happen?" I asked.

"She met a porcupine!"

"I thought that happened yesterday?"

Claudia looked at me as if I had been barfed up by a cat. "It did," she replied. "I knew there was one around but I thought Mipsy had the sense to stay clear of it. I have no idea what happened. I had her tied up so she couldn't have chased anything, I mean, anyway, she should have learned her lesson."

"Ah, yes," I said in an attempt to show a deep understanding of their plight. Claudia was not ready for me to explain that sometimes dogs took a while to learn cause and effect.

Claudia lived on a small farm where she raised sheep. Each morning, after letting Mipsy have a brief run, Claudia tied her to a tree while she attended to any sheep that were in the barn.

"Take her in back," I said, pointing to the treatment room. "And give her a premed,"—a shot to calm the patient before surgery, and hopefully bring a measure of pain relief to this poor suffering dog. "You know the drill."

Porcupine quills are a problem. A common problem. Usually it is a simple matter to remove them, but it requires anesthesia and can be time consuming. It is one of those procedures where, in many cases, we cannot charge the client as much as it costs us in time and drugs to perform.

Mipsy's tangle with the porcupine the day before had been minor. Today's looked far more serious. The wild critter must be getting annoyed.

Mipsy was a bad case. Her tongue and lips were spiked together by the quills. She couldn't pant, she couldn't drink; she looked miserable and forlorn.

I rushed through a couple of routine vaccination cases—fortunately, no reported problems—and went to check on the porcupine victim. Claudia and Nicky had Mipsy unconscious and were pulling quills out with forceps which they then dunked in a bowl of water to wash the vicious little spikes off the instrument. Because her mouth was stapled shut there had been no way to pass a breathing tube into her airway. We do this usually because it allows her to breathe without us choking her while working in the mouth—sometimes quills can be embedded back in the throat—and to stop pieces of broken quills, rinse water, or blood going down the wrong pipe. Also, because removing quills often takes a long time, the breathing tube allows the patient to be kept unconscious with an inhaled anesthetic from which they can wake up quicker. Today we used an injectable anesthetic drug to keep her under until her mouth was 'unstapled' and a tube could be passed. As you can see from my account of her actions, Claudia is a highly trained and skilled professional.

"You must have found a whole family of porcupines," I said a little more brightly than before coffee. Claudia glared at me.

The rest of the day passed in a blur of uneventful routine. At close of business, Claudia headed home. Behind her, at the end of a dangerously stretched leash, Mipsy lumbered from leg to leg, following Claudia's frustrated tugs.

At least she hadn't scooted on the quills.

38

And It's Only Wednesday

With ruin upon ruin, rout on rout,
Confusion worse confounded ~ Paradise Lost, Milton

On Saint Valentine's Day—a day to honor the patron saint of lovers—the wicked, warped reception staff, urged on by the nursing staff, had made sure that all the surgery cases, both dogs and cats, were neuters. They found this extremely funny, screwing their faces into grotesque expressions to demonstrate how men winced and suffered whenever a patient had his manhood downsized.

I won't comment on that.

June had left her reception desk and hovered in my peripheral vision as Claudia arrived—late.

I am fairly slow to rise to surprises—I expect it's an age thing—but at my technician's appearance—once again with a sad faced Mipsy in tow, I was taken aback.

"And what happened this time?"

"Urghh," Claudia replied.

This was a sentiment I fully understood. After all, this was the third day in a row that Mipsy had been shish-kebabed by a Porcupine.

I took a quick look at her. Her condition wasn't quite as bad as before.

"You should be able to pull them out without general anesthesia," I said, then suggested a sedative dose.

Claudia, muttering unvoiced fricatives—a repeated short word, starting with F— glared at me as if I were guilty of some misdeed. After years of marriage and working with over-stressed nurses and technicians, I am a rarity—a man who has learned when to keep quiet. Usually.

"So" she said. "You are blaming me, aren't you?"

I hadn't said a word about blame, but my eyebrows had inched upwards of their own accord when I saw Mipsy, and Claudia had noticed. This must have been my blunder.

"Why don't you come out and say it."

"Okay," I said. "I say it."

"There, I knew you would blame me."

I was adrift in a sea of confusion, bravely trying not to drown in the waves of hostility being sent my way.

"Ah, what is this about?" I said in a tentative voice.

"As if you don't know." She glared at me. "The porcupine, of course."

"Do you want to tell me?"

She stared at me in a way that showed she and her dog thought it was my fault. "It was up the tree all the time," she said at last. As Claudia stomped off towards the kennels, I understood—the tree to which Mipsy had been faithfully tied for the last three days. A smile would have been rash at that moment, but I was about to mutter a soothing banality when, fortunately, June spoke up and saved me.

"You have a live one in room one."

"Yes?" I asked with an interrogative expression – head cocked, eyebrows raised—this time not committing a faux pas.

"You'll see."

I lifted the chart from the holder outside the room—Mr. Palenko with three Dachshund puppies to examine and vaccinate. I tapped on the door and entered.

"Hi, Dr. Kevorkian," the client said.

"Wrong guy," I said, spinning on my heel as if to leave.

With a loud chuckle he extended his hand. I knew him—not too well—he managed the local liquor store. From past experience I knew he was one to banter.

I couldn't resist. "Did you raise these to eat?" I asked.

Sometimes I am amazed at my quick and clever remarks, although I had stolen that one from a teacher I once had who couldn't stand dogs, and I had been waiting years to use it.

"Not these," he said. "These are the short variety. Proper wieners come in longer lengths."

I was lost for a comeback, so instead I tried to look professional.

Tell you the truth, I liked the guy. Humor is often a rare commodity when clients are concerned about their pets, worried about possible illnesses, or dreading their bill. I left, still smiling I think, or trying to, and took the case folder to the front desk. The receptionist, June, busy with a lady at the desk, looked up at me as I placed it beside her.

"You will need another one of those," I said, pointing to the 'new puppy' brochure in her hand, which she was about to pass over the counter. "For Mr. Palenko's pups." Before I could add a clever comment about wieners, a large woman, looking as Friar Tuck would have if, instead of being a friar, he had been a nun of more sober habit, lanced her voice across the waiting room with enough icy disdain to freeze a martini. "You—at the counter—you have monopolized the receptionist for ten minutes."

"Ma'am," June, the receptionist, replied. "This lady is not monopolizing me, I am helping her."

"So what are you doing?"

"My job." June has been known to be—forceful—on suitable occasions.

"Humph. Why haven't I been called? You have seen two others while I have been here."

"Have you registered and signed in?"

"Why?"

"So we know you are here."

"You can see I am here." Clients expecting the staff to second guess them are fortunately rare.

"Why are you here?"

"For my flu shot."

"Pardon?"

"My flu shot. Are you deaf as well as blind?"

"This is a veterinary office. That's why those clients had pets with them. We don't do flu shots."

"So who is this Doctor Hart?"

"He is a veterinarian."

"Why didn't you say so when I came in?"

Her abrupt departure in a flurry of muttered words coincided with my aunt's abrupt and explosive entrance. They barely squeezed through the door together. The fact that Auntie hadn't noticed our outspoken visitor did not bode well for this visit.

"I found a book of yours." My aunt's tone was ominous; her attitude confrontational. "It must be yours."

She slapped a small unimpressive volume on the counter, much like a Knight would throw down a gauntlet. There had been no time to gird my mental loins, as it were, in preparation to meet this surprise assault.

"Why do you say that?" I asked, in a lame but brave riposte.

"Because it is about accidents and emergencies." She added the slap of her hand to the earlier slap of the book. "I looked at it."

"Did you like it?" What she could have learned from it, I couldn't guess.

"I thought it was a text book about emergency medicine." She followed her cryptic comment with a few moments silence. "It's not," she added.

"I know," I said in a weak verbal parry. I mean what else could I say? I had no idea where the conversation was going. On the one hand, I was quite pleased that she appeared to be taking an interest in my work, on the other, I felt the sharp prickle of apprehension that she had a hidden agenda. "Like its title says, it's about Accidents and Emergencies in Anesthesia," I said.

My statement was followed by another meaningful silence.

"Why do you need that?" she asked, in a way that made one feel she had delivered a sermon. It showed me the warning light at the end of the conversational tunnel.

"It's a good way to learn how to avoid them," I said, trying not to yield to an idiotic temptation to throw myself at her feet and beg for forgiveness.

"If you knew your job you wouldn't make mistakes."

"That's my point exactly, Auntie," I replied brightly. "I thought if I learned about them, I would know my job better, and hopefully make fewer mistakes or none at all."

"Oh, there's no point in arguing with you. You are too obtuse."

Obtuse? Did she mean I was slow-witted?

"I can't understand why you ever went into this profession in the first place. After all you have few of the skills that are needed." Then she left as abruptly as had the female friar, I mean nun, because, as even I knew, you cannot have female friars—of course I did.

At least I could be grateful that the waiting room was empty. I did not dare look at Nicky or June. I would be sure to blush, and add to their delight as they watched the family skirmish.

Unfortunately, I was feeling a little the same way about having the skills, or lack thereof, to enter the veterinary profession, because I had recently read a learned journal article by a veterinarian much more eminent in the profession than I, Dr. Jennifer Schori. Amongst the attributes of a veterinarian she had listed:

"Psychologist, behavioralist, diagnostician, surgeon, manager, human resource person, counselor, coach, referee, acrobat (think of the positions we have to get in sometimes for those examinations), public health authority, businessman/woman…the list goes on and on."

Many young people aspire to becoming a veterinarian at some time during their what-should-I-do-with-my-life years, Dr. Schori continued. She pointed out that veterinary medicine has an advantage for those who cannot make up their minds about what to do with their lives, allowing them to chart a course that mixes in a little of everything.

I prefer to think of it as the equivalent of a liberal arts degree in medical science.

Maybe that was what Auntie had implied. After all, in Aunt Josephine's mind my life, starting at birth, had been a succession of sometimes slow, sometimes precipitous descents, Her belief was, I expect, predicated on my lack of her guidance in the fundamentals of life that I should have received during my haphazard development. We had not met until quite far into our relative existences, when we found we were related by marriage. In her view I could not expect to perform to her required level of professionalism and expertise, and my modest successes were merely fortuitous occurrences, quite unconnected to years of study, memorization, learning, repetition or practice.

June awoke me from my reverie, and incidentally, I thought, saved me again from further verbal savaging, this time by Auntie's tongue, not Claudia's. But Auntie had left, so the savaging was of my own imagination.

"Sorry to interrupt, but we are backed up."

We weren't, the waiting room was empty but it's her usual attention getting gambit.

"Now, you really will like this next one," she said. "She's already in a room."

I glanced down at the case notes to buy time—the reason for visit, examination for spay. A straightforward case I thought. I was not expecting mental gymnastics.

The client smiled with devastating teeth. "I'm Mrs. Deland," she said, "I want you to tell me if she is pregnant."

Seated on the chair in the corner of the exam room, the lazy length of her legs told me she was tall. The exposed shoulders suggested that her main source of nutrition came from Sweet and Low. A young Doberman weaved around the legs of chair, exam table and client, its leash a macramé pattern of contact between them. Perhaps the Doberman would use it to find her way back after the examination.

"Ah, I was told you wanted her spayed."

"I only want her spayed if she is pregnant. If she's not, don't spay her because I want her to have puppies."

"Say that again."

"I only want her spayed if she is pregnant. If she's not, don't spay her because I want her to have puppies."

I took a course in logic once. Like my client, it baffled me. Antoine de Saint-Exupery, a favorite author of my childhood, had had the good sense to state that *'Pure logic is the ruin of the spirit.'* I believed him.

"And I need her spayed today because I'm going to a wedding out of town, not mine, and I'm leaving her with my husband, ex, and he wouldn't understand if she was pregnant." That baffled me too. I wasn't sure of the connection. Would he understand if she were spayed?

"She's had nothing to eat since last night." A necessary condition for elective surgery.

What the heck. Kevorkian, the flying nun, Auntie and the logic of spaying. Not yet lunchtime and my neurons were being stretched. And I must not forget Mipsy, our chronic porcupine victim.

Being a coward I passed Mrs. Deland to Claudia with an aside to go over the problems of breeding, and unravel the choice between unknown fatherly parentage—pups she did not want—and breeding a purebred litter. Like many wannabe breeders, she had not done her research on the demand for pups, and the cost. June showed her the flaws in her argument and we admitted the bitch to spay and added it to the neuters.

One day I asked Auntie about it.

"What's the problem," she had answered. "Why didn't you do it?"

"Do what."

"What your client asked."

"Duh."

Somewhere I mislaid that book on Accidents and Emergencies in Anesthesia. We all lose books, or lend them to our friends who don't return them, or put them in a garage sale by mistake. But there are some books whose loss we always remember. The book on Accidents and Emergencies in Anesthesia, now long out of print, is one professional book I regret losing. Although this was about human, not animal anesthesia, the principles are the same for both. This was a detailed catalog of what can go wrong, what not to do, what to avoid, and how to recognize and correct mistakes, by those who had experienced them. I guess it was a record of rough days.

In my own twisted logic, I believed Auntie thought that without a book on anesthetic problems I would be forced to think for myself, and be better off that way. Anyway I am convinced that Aunt Josephine stole it.

I welcomed the end of the day. Mournful Mipsy would go home. I hoped that the porcupine had the good sense to find another tree. As to our other surgical patients, the unfortunate neuter cases, I found no joy in the fact that thanks to their downsized manhood they would never again serenade or woo their true loves in memory of Saint Valentine.

39

The Doberman

The unexpected always happens. ~ 19th Century Proverb.

"I suppose you want me to believe that you never make mistakes." Aunt Josephine may have been speaking of Fidget, her little dog who yapped at me, but I felt this was a follow up from the Accident book. Aunt Josephine obviously wished to protest something.

About to reply along the lines of "I wouldn't say that," I had the sense to hold my own counsel instead. No need to give Auntie any evidence to share with Mrs. Ziglepush for a possible coordinated attack at an imagined slight. I couldn't at the time think how she might use it, but her mind was sufficiently devious to use even my choice of coffee against me if it suited her.

Over the years I have learned a lot from documenting mistakes, some funny, some bizarre, a few really nasty. Not necessarily mine. Some I remember with horror. One in particular, a poor dog who lost his toes to ignorance when someone used their newly acquired electro therapy unit to stop toenails bleeding after they had been clipped short, without first attempting to understand the technique of electro-surgery. Fortunately he did it under anesthesia. The arteries in all the dog's toes thrombosed, and the toes fell off.

"So, are you going to tell me?"

Her interrogation had been prompted, I believed, not only by the book, but by the confusion she had suffered at a previous visit when she was rendered speechless at the sight of one of my more eccentric clients—the one who wrote checks using the reception counter for bust support. Now Auntie was back in the fray, taking up her complaint where she had left off because I had given her little dog a placebo to which she objected.

"If it doesn't do anything for her, why did you charge me for it?"

Good point. I had given her a placebo for an imagined bladder infection—imagined by Aunt Josephine that is—because there was no other way to make her leave the practice. She had to have a vial of pills in her sweaty little hand. Had I not charged her, her suspicions would have been magnified further.

"She recovered didn't she?" Rather a lame reply; one I had used before.

"Humph."

"In Fidget's case, there was no mistake." While she digested that I remembered other nasty situations I had witnessed. The use of an infra-red heating lamp used by a farmer, to keep his pet warm after surgery to remove an infected uterus. It slipped to within a few inches of her body—for twenty minutes only—enough to severely burn her from the point of her shoulder to her hip.

The there were bandages that were wrapped too tightly, or got wet, shrank, and strangled the circulation. A few problems I can boast that I had helped remedy, like assisting a recent graduate who had dropped an artery during a spay. As a rule I don't admit which were my mistakes, except for one, which I clearly remember after forty years, and sincerely regret.

"Ah, so you have made mistakes." By not categorically denying any possible sleight of hand with Fidget I had left myself open to covering up errors in all my other cases.

"Yes," I said. "I had once had a rare reaction to a tranquillizer drug that slowed the heart so severely that the dog lost consciousness—fortunately easily remedied—with prompt injection of another drug."

"Is that all?"

"Once I was examining a dog that sat down as I took its temperature and broke the thermometer. That left glass fragments in a rather inaccessible place, which was a little awkward. And there were funny ones, Auntie, if you have a warped sense of humor, like the Schnauzer who turned bright yellow from being dipped in the wrong concentration of lime dip to treat mange. It didn't hurt him, but it sure took a lot of effort, soap, peroxide, and most other available cleaning solutions before we had him restored to his normal mealy-gray color."

"I don't think that's funny."

Why am I not surprised? She wouldn't be satisfied until she heard the worst. So I told her about the Doberman.

A Doberman pinscher was diagnosed with a tumor on his larynx. To help the surgeon reach the tumor, after anaesthetizing the patient I performed a tracheotomy, made a hole in its neck, through which I continued the anesthesia. The surgery went smoothly. I stayed with the dog until he had recovered consciousness enough to sit up, then left, confident all would be fine with the patient. Some time that night he vomited, a not unusual sequel to anesthesia. But, not realizing that he was breathing through a tracheotomy, he lay down with the tracheotomy opening in the vomit. He blocked his airway and suffocated.

It is not a case I like to remember. It is not a case I can forget.

Auntie didn't say anything for some moments. For the first time I caught a fleeting emotion of sadness. "That must be a difficult memory," she said quietly. "I am sorry. I didn't mean to.... After that, I don't think I'll worry about Fidget's medicine. And at my last visit, that woman, the one at the desk with the check—I understand that you can't always choose your clients."

She left my sails windless.

40

Thursday—Day of Rest

(Aut viam inveniam aut faciam) Either I shall find a way, or I shall make one. ~ Hannibal

Children are the mirrors reflecting our early behavior. Lest you have forgotten, here is a short tale that June told us, about Ricky, her three-year-old son.

Tiny Turtle Talk
Oh, Oh.
"Mommy. Mommy. Look."
"It's a baby turtle. Where did you find it?"
Ricky pointed towards the back yard.
"In the pond?"
Ricky nodded. His face gleamed with a huge smile at the pride in his discovery.
"The one behind our house?" June asked.
"Uh-huh."
"You have to put him back in the pond, dear."
"No!" Ricky stamped his foot. "He's mine."
Ricky dragged a chair to the sink, climbed up and started to run cold water.
"What are you doing?" June asked.
Ricky looked at her and then put the turtle in the water.
"Oh no. He can't stay here. Anyway that's our kitchen sink, not a turtle pond."
"No."
"But he's only a baby dear. He will miss his Mommy."

"No."
"He will be happier in the pond."
"He won't. "
"He'll miss his friends."
"I'm his friend."
"You put it back!"
"No!"
"He will be lonely."
"He's mine."

June picked up the phone and called a friend. "Alice, I need your help. Ricky has found this baby turtle in the pond and won't put it back. I'm not happy. What if it's infected with salmonella?"

"What do you think I can do?" Alice said.

"Could you talk to him?"

"If he won't listen to you, he's not going to listen to me."

"I've got it. You call him and say you are the turtle's mother. Tell him he has to come home.'

"Are you nuts? He knows my voice, and anyway I'd get the giggles."

"Alice, can't you think of *anything?*"

Then it was Alice's turn for inspiration. "What if I have my mother call? Ricky doesn't know her."

"Hi Ricky, this is Mrs. Turtle, baby turtle's mommy, the one's who's visiting with you. I really miss him and would like him to come home now."

"Where do *you* live?"

"In the large pond behind your house."

"I didn't see you."

"I was out visiting."

"Where's his daddy?"

"He's on vacation in another pond."

"Must he come home now?"

"Yes, because it's nearly time for his supper."

"Will I be able to visit?"

"He'll always be here. I'm sure you will see him again."

In the silence, Ricky's face crumpled, but he shed no tears. He held onto the phone, baby turtle held firmly in his other hand. Ricky and the turtle looked at each other for a few moments.

"Okay, I guess," Ricky said quietly.

41

Frantic Friday

The moment there is suspicion about a person's motives, everything he does becomes tainted. ~ Mohandas Gandhi

"So why didn't you use the Heimlich maneuver?"

What a question. Ah, TGIF had been so close. Late Friday afternoon, and the beer in the fridge beckoned. Time to savor a few moments at the end of the week, review the highs and lows and put the debris of the day behind us. Patients treated and saved. Clients happy. Appointments cleared, cages empty, all calls returned. There had remained but a quick thrust of a finger, already poised over the answering machine switch, when the telephone rudely interrupted our reveries. June answered, listened, turned to me. "You might want to hear this." That meant this is definitely for you.

"I need something for my dog, Maggie, she's lost her bark." The voice owned a beautiful long haired Retriever.

"When did this happen?"

"About three days ago. She started drooling. Still tries to eat but spits it out. She's happy enough. Wags her tail, but snores terrible if she moves much. I didn't want to let it go through the weekend."

"Right."

"Glad I caught you."

My reply was of course remarkably restrained under the circumstances. My belief that this pet had left a more positive impression with us than his owner was being reinforced. But a client he was, and we were still in the office. We shelved the idea of the beer. June and my new nurse, Nicky, who had completed her first week with us, volunteered to hang around hoping to plunder the adult beverages in the fridge a bit later. After all this was Nicky's first TGIF.

We saw the client and patient as soon as they arrived. Lying quietly on the exam room floor, alert and tail-wagging, Maggie waited for the verdict. She was not short of breath, and was making no significant effort to breathe. Saliva dribbled in sticky strips from the side of her mouth. I patted her and checked the elasticity of her skin—perhaps a little dehydrated.

The owner was restless.

I started the examination at the front and worked back down the body. Not far. Aha. A thickened mass in her throat. Super-sleuth palpated the offending mass. Maggie gagged.

"Let's take a look, shall we?"

I tried to open her mouth. Maggie gagged again. As she 'opened wide' and stretched her head in a futile attempt to up-chuck, I glimpsed something in her throat.

A ball: A tennis ball!

"I think she tried to swallow a ball," I said brightly.

"Wondered where it went," the owner replied. "What are you going to do about it?"

The ball was lodged in the back of her throat, behind the end of the soft palate, in front of the entrance to her windpipe, and obstructing the airflow from her nose.

"No wonder she is snoring," I observed brightly, ignoring for the moment explaining what I could do, so he didn't see my indecision while I wrestled nobly with the alternatives.

At rest, she was comfortable. There was however no doubt that she would need anesthesia to remove it, and that awakened the memory.

In a similar case reported long before in the literature, a

veterinarian intended to remove a ball lodged in the same place where Maggie had the offending obstruction, by making an incision under the throat. As he made the skin incision, the patient, relaxed by the anesthetic, obligingly let the ball fall out through the mouth. He had merely to stitch the skin together and wake the patient up.

However as he had estimated the charges including emergency surgery, and loathe to present a bill for less as it was after hours, he did not tell the owners of the easy resolution. He charged them the full estimate. His guilt must have been evident because next day they had their unfortunate pooch examined by their regular veterinarian who found one layer of stitches—those in the skin—and no signs of any further surgery. They complained to the licensing board. He was found guilty of conduct unbecoming to the profession, fined, and his license revoked.

With this in mind, I planned, after ushering her into the twilight world of dreams, to make my first attempt through the mouth. Smart choice don't you think?

One is of course between a rock and a hard place in such a case—remove the object, but don't suffocate the patient trying! With the patient completely relaxed the ball might fall out, but it could as easily act like a valve when she tried to breathe in, and close off her airway. While I placed a catheter in a vein, to give fluids, and to have access to her circulation if I needed to make any heroic efforts to resuscitate the dog, I allowed her to breathe oxygen gently through a mask. This would replace the air in her lungs and give me a precious few minutes before she asphyxiated if things did not go according to plan, or if my actions blocked her airway. And it gave June time to ransack the cupboards for a large enough pair of forceps.

I had been faced with this problem in a kitten not long before—a middle-of-the-night call. The unfortunate wretch had a piece of gristle stuck in her throat, much like the ball.

Unfortunately she had not been as stoic and cooperative as Maggie.

In obvious distress the poor little kitty would not tolerate a mask, but focused on breathing as she was, I was able, with divine help I believe, to inject a tad of anesthetic into a vein.

I frantically tried to remove the object with forceps. It shredded. All I could do was pull pieces off it. She went blue, and her heart stopped. Throwing caution to the winds I squeezed her throat while trying to grip it again with the forceps. I think the instrument merely pushed her soft palate out of the way, but the gristle popped out. With the airway open I started immediate CPR—again somewhat frantically. A wave of relief swept over me as the kitten's tongue and gums turned pink. A heart beat returned. Moments later she gasped, and started the road to recovery. It had been so close.

I allowed Maggie to continue breathing the oxygen. I played for all the time I could get.

"What are you waiting for?" the owner asked. Demanded really.

Ignoring him, I injected a reversible anesthetic into Maggie's intravenous catheter, watched her relax, and give a sigh. I peered down her throat wondering how she had swallowed anything so large. Could I hope to remove it this way? With my new nurse holding open the jaws, I reached down with a large spatula and tried to push the palate up over the ball. In the other hand I held forceps designed to help deliver puppies, a bit like barbecue tongs, fancier and a lot more expensive, but that's as close as I can describe. As I pulled, I had June squeeze Maggie's throat behind the ball. It worked. Out it came. The doing was much easier than the anticipation.

"If you could see it, why did you have to sedate her?" he asked. "My other vet took a stuck bone out of her mouth, and everything, without sedation." That took me by surprise. I was still glowing with the success of the procedure.

"I didn't want to take the risk of her choking," I said.

"So why didn't you use the Heimlich maneuver?"

"It wouldn't have helped to force out something that size," I said.

"You kept her waiting. It was an emergency. My dog was choking."

I did not say anything about the three days the ball had been stuck, and the fact that he merely thought she had lost her bark. He was now thinking about the cost, so his attitude had the implied threat of a complaint that I had not been concerned enough.

Putting aside nasty thoughts of adding an exasperation factor to the bill, a PIA surcharge, and a needed drink factor, I reversed the anesthetic. Maggie was none the worse for wear and was promptly shipped home. He had no check book, and no cash on hand—it was an emergency you understand.

I choked back the urge to pad the bill.

42

Saturday Morning

It's not rocket surgery. ~ Anonymous

Not a breath of air stirred. The mercury and humidity climbed in fits and starts like kittens on a lace curtain. Fans whirred, brows dripped, patients panted. Even client's checks were limp. It was a summer Saturday in upstate New York in a month when the full moon had lasted longer than usual.

Office calls and phones calls wrestled each other for the receptionist's attention.

"His nose was swollen yesterday, but it's all better now. What caused it?"

"You can step into room two now, Sir. Sir, Sir! With your dog!"

"You have to bathe him today. I can only come on a Saturday, I have to work you know!"

"Miss, the floor's all wet over here."

Routine double booked shots for *distemperment*, emergency worms, and week old lacerations were interrupted from time to time by dogs shished and kebabed on porcupine quills, fresh cut pads, and animals bumped by inconsiderate vehicles. Then as often happens on a Saturday, the office cleared. We waited, as usual, for the other shoe to drop.

We waited for a good sixty minutes after our normal office hours should have closed, because there was a German shepherd puppy with a broken leg to be discharged that had not yet been picked up.

One might say a routine Saturday morning.

Hot and uncomfortable, with cat and dog hair sticking to face and arms, I thought unprintable thoughts of St. Francis who started this whole ludicrous business. Then the shoe dropped, a pair actually, high heels, on a walk-in client.

I placed the owner's breed and temperament immediately—a generic upscale commuterist, BMW, townhouse, designer teeth. Tres chic. Dressed almost correctly. Her body, not surprisingly, almost embarrassingly exposed due to her struggle to carry a mediocre sized five to six month old Schnauzer puppy. She stopped at the front desk, murmured her problem. As I wrote up a record that had slipped my mind, I caught snatches of her conversation with the receptionist.

Her puppy was grinding his teeth! This an emergency? I welcomed the challenge.

In exasperation I indicated to the front desk that it was fine to take her. A tooth-grinding emergency couldn't take that long to examine, soothe and reassure. Anyway I must still discharge the puppy with the broken leg whose owner was on her way, a complete ditz, hair dyed blonde to highlight her IQ, and not nearly as interesting as this walk-in client. I do not usually refer to clients like this, but you might gather that by this time I was beginning to lose my habitual bonhomie.

This presenting complaint I added to my improbable emergency file, with other such gems as "My cat is purring too loud," "My puppy is sticking his tongue out at me," "My Parakeet's just landed in my peas," all considered by the owners to be good valid reasons for an after hour's office call.

The pup lay quietly on the exam table. It appeared a bit depressed. I stroked it to establish contact and found to my surprise that his skin was not as loose, not as supple as it should be. Pinched gently between the fingers the skin stayed tented, the normal elasticity reduced. This pup was dehydrated. The owner volunteered that he hadn't been eating or drinking for at least three days—since he started to grind his teeth.

The pup resented having his jaws handled. Ha! I deduced a problem in the mouth! Gently persuading the critter to open wide, the owner and I bumped heads, jostled for position, peered inside together, expecting to see perhaps some foreign object lodged in the teeth. I was aware of her Shalimar and perhaps a little distracted by the inadequate struggle of her halter-top.

Surprise! The pup was losing his baby teeth to the inexorable push of his permanent dentition, but he did have a problem. The loosened upper cheek teeth on each side were tilted sideways preventing the pup from closing his mouth properly. He ground his teeth to relieve the discomfort. Each time he did he made his gums bleed. Halter-top did a mock swoon and sat in the chair conveniently provided.

It would be some days before the offending baby teeth were loose enough to fall out of their own accord.

"I agree," I said brightly, my voice rising with surprise. "This really is an emergency."

"Really!" she said in a way that confirmed her assessment of my ignorance. She knew that teeth grinding was *always* an emergency medical problem. Of course, I really knew that too.

I planned to keep the little critter with me at least overnight, soon had him on fluids, anesthetized, and the offending teeth removed. The owner would call later for a progress report. So much for the start to Saturday afternoon. At that moment the German shepherd's owner breezed in—you remember my telling you about the one who was on her way?

We had first seen her dog a month before when it had fallen from a second floor window. Being young and elastic in the way of young puppies—and lucky—it had bounced off the sidewalk none the worse for wear. Then two days ago she had brought it in again. With the same complaint. This time it *had* broken its leg in the fall. Now it sported a metal pin in its leg and a bright red designer padded bandage.

"Now then," I said brightly as I showed her to the door, "You must keep your windows closed. For the pup's sake."

"Really," she said, her voice and eyebrows rising with the question. "Why? Mustn't he be in a draft?"

43

Skunk Pursuit

But screw your courage to the sticking place, and we'll not fail. ~
Macbeth, William Shakespeare

Aunt Josephine needed to check up on me. It had been some years since we had seen each other. Helen and I had moved, in fits and starts, to upstate New York. As we now owned a Bed & Breakfast we felt obliged to offer her safe harbor for her stay, or a short part of it. She accepted.

I checked my horoscope frequently for auspicious signs that she still had me in mind to benefit from her will. She had conferred numerous other benefits on me over the years, of a wisdom-like nature, why not other gifts?

Helen and I lived on about eight acres in a long valley flanked by low hills. About a hundred yards behind the house the land rose steeply to the property boundary at the top of the hill. The left side was dominated by a thick stand of trees, our own private wood. A series of three terraces broke up the slope on the right. Upstate New York is admirably endowed with four footed wildlife—deer, raccoons, possums, and skunks—and we had our fair share. Twice we had seen deer giving birth on the lower terrace. Wild turkeys frequently came to within a few yards of the house. Foxes and coyotes were occasional visitors. One evening we watched in delight as a raccoon showed us off to her litter by climbing up with them to peer in the ground-floor windows of the sitting and dining rooms.

During the first few days of Aunt Josephine's stay, we

had been troubled by a feral cat which had placed our property on his territorial list. Although he was quiet, his nocturnal visits were met with yodeling from our kitty, Oliver, to the alarm and consternation of our B&B guests. This stranger had to be removed.

One Sunday afternoon, free of visitors, and while Aunt Josephine was exploring the neighboring village with another guest, we set a humane Have-a-Heart trap for the nocturnal visitor. Baited with aged tuna fish, we placed it behind the laundry room. Then, duties over, my wife and I went for a walk.

When we returned we saw a black and white animal in the trap.

"Looks like we have us a cat," I said.

We edged closer. "More like a skunk," Helen replied.

Helen was none to keen to encourage a closer encounter with the little animal. She still had memories of a late night encounter many years before, despite my assurances that the smell had gone—even when she got wet. So, after we had decided that the cat really was a skunk, we enjoyed a brief break for adult refreshment and to gather our disjointed wits.

With courage screwed to wherever it would most likely stick, I advanced on the trap holding before me a blanket, a sacrifice that could be burned if the need arose, thinking of all the sundry advice I had learned over the years about the habits of skunks. None of it from Aunt Josephine.

"It has to be able to lift its tail to spray, so you stuff it in a tube, like a narrow drain pipe." How?

"You should tranquillize it, then haul it out of the trap, pronto." Oh yeah?

"Crawl up to it slowly, so it is not threatened, and it will be fine." Fine for what?

"Approach from the front. They can't see clearly, and while he figures out who you are, you grab him." Then what happens?

Having chewed, swallowed and digested the advice, I

threw the blanket over the trap and leaped back. An inspired move. So far so good. Then, the darned animal tried to pull the blanket into the trap through the wire.

A sage, far wiser than I, once said that if handed a lemon, make lemonade. What does one make of a skunk? As we watched, we realized that the skunk, with his little paws and teeth, was making the best of *his* situation. All we had in our favor was the blanket, and that he couldn't see us. Maybe, if he was busy with the blanket, he wouldn't figure out what we were doing, so I helped push more folds of the blanket into the trap with a stick. When he had covered himself to his satisfaction he curled up and went to sleep and I took the opportunity to sneak up, as quiet as any Indian scout, and release the door to give him his freedom. He preferred to sleep. Now what?

In a bold and courageous move I decided to pull the blanket out and step away. Fortunately skunks really are short sighted, and despite being rudely awakened, he merely peered myopically at the receding blanket, until his recognized his naked condition and crawled out of the trap. I retreated before his approach, but ignoring me, he waddled in his skunk like way around the house and into the drainage ditch where he sought shelter under a culvert.

We celebrated with another early afternoon Scotch because it was the weekend. We were still congratulating ourselves on our heroic action when Auntie returned. She was due to leave next day. To my surprise, I was almost reluctant to see her go.

Next morning, we were loading the car with her sundry bags and souvenirs when she came out of the house. At that moment the skunk chose to waddle up from the ditch. He had reached the middle of the lawn before he noticed Auntie. They both froze. The skunk's nose twitched. He swept his head left and right sizing up the opposition. Auntie stayed rooted to the spot. The skunk blinked first. It turned and ran. Ran from Auntie!

She saw me watching. Her Auntie frown returned.

"Don't you dare…" she said, giving me her best glare.

We both understood what she meant. Oh, what power at last, after all those years. Not a word, Auntie, not a word. Until now. Because, you know, I never promised to keep quiet. Looking back, I really enjoyed her visit.

44

I am Oliver, and I am a Cat.

Transcribed, at my whim, by my guardian.

Which if not victory is yet revenge. ~ Milton

    I felt I should give the last word to Oliver. He is my feline mentor, advisor, and all round family elder on whom I rely for the paw of approval, and at fifteen he deserves to be honored as a patriarch, as I am honored to be a member of his family. And, I well remember what Anne taught me years ago, a cat can communicate most effectively when it deigns to.

    He knows that I have told you about pets, staff, clients, and the improbable situations in which we sometimes find ourselves. So when he addressed me one morning recently, I felt obliged to lend an ear.

    "If your pets could write about you, what do you think they would say?" He was lecturing me in the interval between my awakening and filling his food dish. This was obviously a direct challenge for me to ask what *he* would say. As our friend Will said, "Ay, there's the rub."

    "You'd have to tame a cockroach to write for you, Like Mehitabel has done," I replied, trying to confuse him. I referred of course to *archy and mehitabel*, by don marquis, (the lowercase is deliberate), where archy the cockroach transcribes mehitabel's stories—using lower case only because he can't hit the shift key. I was sure I had puzzled Oliver by my intellectual reference.

"I don't need an Archie, I have you."

"Touché." I paused a second, after all I still wasn't quite awake. "How do you know about Archie and Mehitabel?"

"I am Oliver, and I am a cat. As you should know, that makes me omniscient. I can trace my family back to the ancient Gods of Egypt. Can you say the same?"

"Well, they had to be ancient in those days, didn't they?" He glared at me and scooped up another piece of food with his paw. I gave in. "So what would you say?"

He carefully chewed and swallowed before replying.

"My owner loves me; he would do anything for me, as long as my tail is cut off, my ears cropped for his vanity, my toes declawed. Oh, and he cut my balls off."

"Oliver! No one has touched your ears and tail."

"I speak for all pets," he said, with a condescending tilt of his head.

"If you speak for all pets," I replied, "Perhaps you should say, 'She stayed by me in the hurricane and risked her life for me? Or he shares my food because he can not afford anything else, and he will not abandon me.'" I thought I had him there because he ignored me, so I went on. "During Hurricane Katrina, the Federal Emergency Management Agency, FEMA, didn't allow people to take their animals with them. Half of those who stayed behind in New Orleans did so because they wouldn't abandon their pets, even when their own lives were in severe danger."

He sniffed. I had obviously bested him with that reply, so he again ignored me.

"My direct ancestor Mafdet was the first Egyptian feline goddess," he said. It was if I hadn't spoken. "But the most famous was Bastet. She was not only a household goddess, protector of women, children and domestic cats, but she was also the goddess of sunrise, music, dance, pleasure, as well as family, fertility and birth."

"She needed her God-like powers to prevent being overwhelmed with obligations," I quipped.

"Don't be facetious. Anyway, she made sure that the penalty for killing a cat—even accidentally—was death. If a house caught on fire, the cats were rescued before the people, as it should be!"

"Not all Egyptian Gods were cats. What about Anubis?"

"That jackal-headed dog? Elevating him to divine status was idiotic. But that happened before they realized that the *first cat* was the daughter of Isis, and the goddess for the moon and the sun. They even, showing great wisdom I might add, built a whole city for cat worship, Bubastis, in honor of Bastet."

"So why did medieval Europeans believe cats were in league with the Devil?" I said. "Cats were burned along with witches."

"Some of *your* ancestors weren't so bright."

"Wasn't Bubastis that depraved place where thousands of pilgrims sang silly songs, drank wine, prayed and showed their wild behavior at an annual Bubastis Oktoberfest?"

Again he ignored my comments.

"Unfortunately, this city was destroyed by the unthinking Persians in 350 BC," he said.

"You left us with a dubious legacy. Young humans have adopted the behavior of Bastet's worshippers. We call it *Spring Break.*"

His tail twitched reflecting possible annoyance despite his outward appearance of calm control.

"In America, in his century, I admit we at last recognize that our relationship to our pets, to you, has undergone a profound change," I said. "We acknowledge the love between us, and can no longer be called mere *owners.*"

"You never have been." He sounded a little petulant. "At least not where we cats are concerned."

"May I remind you that we let your more recent ancestors into our homes?" I said. "We of all the animal species have developed a close relationship with other species. We have created the human-animal bond."

"The animal-human bond was a mutual arrangement. But it is often bondage—for the animal. Some you keep in bondage to raise for food; some to work. And some you support only for vanity. Those are the ones you call pets."

What is a pet, I mused? A pet is a domesticated animal kept for pleasure rather than utility, and we should note that the verb, *to pet*, expresses fondness, or means to stroke gently or lovingly. It is said that it can also mean a fit of peevishness, sulkiness or anger. At first I thought that was propaganda, but after listening to Oliver I was no longer sure.

He went on without waiting for a reply. "Dogs and cats are the only two animals that you let freely into your homes, and allow to become members of your families. Farm animals, birds or exotic pets are still captives."

Pets do reflect the Ying and Yang of our special relationship with species other than our own.

They highlight the best and the worst of human behavior. As we need ugliness to appreciate beauty, sin to appreciate good, hate to appreciate love, so we need our special relationship to our pets to provide us with a mirror to our own soul. Which of us can look into our pet's eyes and deny this? I daren't admit this to Oliver. Not yet.

"We cats domesticated *you*," he said.

"Your ancestors joined us to feed on the vermin in grain silos," I protested.

"They were pests surrounding your homes."

"What?"

"You had a filthy existence until we took over vermin control for you."

"Well, dogs developed a *symbiotic* relationship with us, guarding us and hunting for us in return for food and shelter." I didn't want to add that this relationship is so close that the dog breeds we have so diligently bred cannot exist without human friendship—anymore than we can exist without theirs—but Oliver beat me to it.

"Your family house-cat can fend for itself, hunt for

food and adapt to a wild environment. Can you see a Shi Tzu, Pug or miniature Yorkie doing the same?"

"You have a point," I conceded. I tried to picture Dammit hunting for food—she would never have had time, she would have been too busy eating.

"And you should bear in mind," he wagged his tail for emphasis. "There are as many feral cats in this country as those in your houses."

"Feral cats are a damn nuisance."

"If you got rid of them, the country would be overrun by rodents."

I quickly changed the subject. I didn't think it polite to talk about trapping his distant relatives. I do have some sensitivity.

"We view our *bond* differently now, and use terms like *companion, guardian,* and *steward,* instead of owner," I said. The loss of human and animal life during Hurricane Katrina had helped us recognize this need.

"On October 6th 2006, President Bush signed the PETS Act (Pets Evacuation and Transportation Standards), into law," I added. "States must have animal evacuation protocols in order to get disaster preparedness funds from FEMA, and allow FEMA to pay for shelters, for both animals and their guardians, in an emergency."

The Fritz Institute predicted that the PETS Act would save thousands of animal and human lives. It has already. Before hurricane Gustav, the authorities in New Orleans organized the Louisiana Mega Shelter which housed more than 1000 animals—cats, dogs, rabbits, lizards, snakes and turtles. Ninety-five percent of evacuees—1.9 million people—were able to take their pets with them when they left.

Oliver interrupted my train of thought.

"It's time for a nap." He leaped onto the windowsill and gave a grunt, meaning I should move things so he could lie in the sun.

"What I do for you," I said.

He stretched, rubbing his face on the sill to claim ownership, and sighed with tuna baited breath.

"One last thought I might write down for you. I think it's about time you learned the truth about us," he said. "And a little about dogs. Puppies and Kittens are really alien invaders, sent to subjugate earth. Their role is to win your affection, and overcome you with love. Then the puppies grow into dogs to police you, and the kittens grow into cats to govern you."

The alien thing seemed far-fetched, and I thought I saw him wink, but the rest of what he said had a ring of truth.

"You can leave me now," he said. "It's time for a nap."

I crept away quietly so as not to disturb him. I had to write his thoughts down before I forgot them; after all, although I was letting him have the last word, he doesn't have an Archie.

Printed in Great Britain
by Amazon